A History of
CHALFONT ST. PETER
and
GERRARDS CROSS

BLACKETTS.

The Feld.

CHALFONT ST. PETER. DETACHED.

DOGGETTS.

DOGGETTS HILL.

DRAPERSLAND.

PHILIPSHILL.

PORTERS.

NEWLAND.

Hurnwick.

GORELANDS.
MANTLES.
ASHWELLS.

CHALFONT ST. GILES.

KIPPINGS.
LITTLE COBWELL.

MEANFIELD.

PINNESTE

Redland.

SILESDEN RIVER-MISBURNE OLD MEAD. DENE ACRE DEMLAND

Chalfont Wasteland

Turvilles.

SHIRELANE.

DEAN FIELD.

Temple Mead
Turners Mead

COMMONDOWN.
SCOLEBURY.
LAYTERS.
OLD FIELD.

GOLD HILL.

THE GRANGE ZERESLAND.

CAMPIONS MEAD.

BULSTRODES.

MATTOCKS
Diddesworth
MORES.

PITLANDS.

BIRCHLAND.
STAMPWELL.

TO OXFORD.

Hatch Riding.

Hoggepresss

MUMFORDS.

WAYS.
MAINT.

Uptonsfield.

Smiths Heath.

OAK END.

MARSHAM

Shaperesden.

CHALFONT ST. PETER.

A SKETCH MAP SHOWING PLACES
MENTIONED IN MEDIEVAL RECORDS.

0.  ¼.  ½.  ¾.  1 MILL.                    2 MILE.

SCALE    OF MILES.

CONJECTURAL NAMES IN ITALICS.
BOUNDARIES: CHALFONT ST. PETER. ＿‧＿‧＿‧＿
                    OAK END. ＿ ＿ ＿ ＿

TO LONDON.

1.

# A History of
# CHALFONT ST. PETER
## and
# GERRARDS CROSS

G. C. Edmonds M.A.

COLIN  SMYTHE
Gerrards Cross 1968

A number of local concerns have generously supported this book and the publishers have asked them to give an outline of their own history and development and services to this community. They have been arranged alphabetically on the last pages.

Made and printed in Great Britain by
The Garden City Press Limited
Letchworth, Hertfordshire

# FOREWORD

This little book, the work of an amateur, owes much to the knowledge and encouragement of many friends. In particular, I wish to express my indebtedness to Mrs. E. M. Elvey and her article on 'The Abbot of Missenden's Estates in Chalfont St. Peter', and to her and the Buckinghamshire Archaeological Society for permission to reproduce her map; to the President (E. Clive Rouse Esq., F.S.A.) and the Secretary (Dr. Audrey Baker) of the Chalfont St. Peter and Gerrards Cross History Society; and to Mr. and Mrs. John Bennell. I hope that some of the fruits of Mr. Bennell's careful studies will soon be published. Mr. Eric Davis and Mr. Veazey, of the County Record Office, have been unfailingly helpful.

I am especially grateful to Mrs. Margaret Noble for typing the manuscript; to Mr. Richard Harman, of the Blandford Press, for his kind interest in its publication, and to my wife for reading and correcting the manuscript and proofs.

There is much yet to be discovered about the history of these villages. Those who wish to pursue further any aspect of it are recommended to avail themselves of the help of the County Museum and County Record Office at Aylesbury, and of the local History Society, whose secretary, Miss Baker, lives at Carey House, Orchehill Avenue, Gerrards Cross.

G. C. E.
1964

The welcome demand for a second edition has given me the opportunity to correct some errors, insert some additional material, and add some notes and references.

The notes will make plain my indebtedness to some other friends besides those mentioned above, but I must also add here my thanks to the sympathetic publishers of this edition, Colin Smythe Limited.

I am indebted to Mr. Clive Rouse for the prints of Chalfont Park and Bulstrode Park : to the Bucks Archaeological Society for the print of Bulstrode House : to Mr. L. Chalenor for the photograph of the Misbourne : and to Mr. J. Gates for the photograph of the workmen who built St. James's Church. The photographs of Chalfont St. Peter Church and village are from old postcards.

I am also indebted to Mr. John Harris of the R.I.B.A. for the print of the Grotto; to the Bucks Record Office for permission to reproduce part of John Fisher's map; and to Mr. John Warren for the photograph of the Darrell tomb.

1968

# INTRODUCTION

This book attempts to set out something of the story of Chalfont St. Peter and Gerrards Cross. Of course, history cannot really be fenced off so neatly as this; these two villages have always had, as they have now, many links with the towns and villages round about. Amersham ('Agmondesham', as it used to be) was our market town; many families had members and lands in both Chalfont St. Peter and Chalfont St. Giles; Gerrards Cross had many associations with Denham, Iver ('Evre'), Fulmer ('Fugelmere') and Hedgerley ('Huggeley' or 'Hegeley'). But for reasons of time and space, it seemed best to resist temptations to wander into neighbouring parishes. Fortunately there are, besides County Histories and several books on 'The Chilterns' and 'The Penn Country', published histories of Denham, Iver, and Fulmer, and of Chalfont St. Giles Church, for those who wish to go further.[1]

But first let us see what the parishes of Chalfont St. Peter and Gerrards Cross *are*.

# CHALFONT ST. PETER AND GERRARDS CROSS

Chalfont St. Peter is an ancient village, Gerrards Cross a newcomer. The ecclesiastical parish of Gerrards Cross was formed in 1859, but it did not become a civil parish until 1895. It was formed by taking pieces out of five parishes – Chalfont St. Peter, Iver, Fulmer, Upton and Langley Marish. There is still a stone by the Oxford Road (not far from St. James's Church) which marks the spot where the parishes of Chalfont St. Peter and Fulmer met. Chalfont St. Peter is a large parish still; but for most of its life it extended from a point beyond Chorley Wood to a little south of the Oxford Road. 'Gerrards Cross Common' was 'Chalfont Heath', and adjoined 'Fulmer Heath'.[2]

## EARLY DAYS

From Camp Road, Gerrards Cross, a path leads to an open space bought by the Parish Council for the benefit of the public. This quiet and pleasant field fringed with trees, and surrounded by high banks and ditches, is the Bulstrode Camp, the largest fortified earthwork in the county. It appears to have been not a permanent home but a place of refuge. On the sides of the valleys round about, many flint implements have been found; and we may imagine the Iron Age inhabitants of this part of

9

Bucks. laboriously building these defences with such primitive tools, and then, when enemy tribes approached, hastily gathering their families and their cattle into this place of refuge. 'Bulstrode' first appears as 'Burstrod' (with a short 'u') and the place-name authorities tell us that it means 'the marsh belonging to the fort'.[3]

There are few streams on this side of the Chilterns, and many dry valleys. As local gardeners know well, the soil is stony, and water quickly drains away. Mr. J. F. Head, in his valuable book, 'Early Man in South Buckinghamshire' shows how sparse are the signs of settlements in prehistoric times: and even of Roman occupation there is little evidence, apart from a few coins, and remains of Roman pottery kilns at Fulmer and Hedgerley. There are pockets of clay and brick-earth hereabouts which have encouraged the manufacture of bricks, tiles and pottery all through the centuries.

By one of the few streams, Chalfont grew up. The Misbourne River is not a very large river, and from time to time it disappears altogether; but it is still a charming stream when it sparkles in the sunlight. It flows through a pleasant valley from Missenden to Denham, and it has watered our beasts and turned our mills through many generations.

The name 'Chalfont', the authorities tell us, comes from 'Ceadeles Funta' or 'Ceadel's spring', 'Ceadel' being a personal name (as in 'Chaddleworth', Berks.). Mr. Head writes: 'The features that repelled settlement and cultivation in early Saxon times were, as might be expected, attractive to outlaws, political exiles, or other refugees. Romano-Britons in rebellion, or unable to adjust themselves to changed conditions, may well have found this hilly no-man's land a welcome retreat. And in this connection it will be recalled that the Place-Name Society, in their Bucks. volume, tell us that each part of the name Chalfont – Ceadeles funta – is of British origin.'

# DOMESDAY AND AFTER

When William the Conqueror sent out his commissioners in 1086 to make a detailed survey of his realm, they found that 'Chalfont' had already been split into two parts (later known as 'St. Giles' and 'St. Peter'). In both there were small organised communities: and the irregular boundary between them shows that outlying settlements were already in existence when, in Saxon times, that boundary was determined. It seems probable that that half-mile of the Misbourne Valley round about 'Oak End' had also originally been part of Chalfont, but had early been taken by a free tenant into the parish of Iver.

No doubt the village of Chalfont St. Peter first grew up by the Misbourne and around Gold Hill Common; but the figures given in the Domesday Survey suggest that already by that time new clearings in the forests were being made and new fields put under the plough in the higher lands. Two roads skirted the parish – Shire Lane, an ancient track which still for several miles forms the boundary between Buckinghamshire and Hertfordshire, and the medieval London-to-Oxford road, still more or less followed by the A40; and, as we shall see, scattered farms and hamlets sprung up near these two roads.

The village was one of the many which William granted to his doughty half-brother, Bishop Odo, from whom it was held, feudal-fashion, by one of his knights, Roger d'Anquetil. Roger was the ancestor of the family of Turville, who held many lands in Bucks. and whose name is still recalled in 'Weston Turville'. In that tough but pious age, when many churches were built and many monasteries founded, one of the Turvilles built a church in our Chalfont, which was dedicated to St. Peter. In 1196 Richard de Turville gave it to the Augustinian Abbey, of Missenden, which had been founded sixty years earlier. In the same period a church was built in 'the other Chalfont' dedicated to St. Giles, and bestowed upon Bradwell Priory.[4]

In the same period, again, the Knights Templars, that famous Order, formed at the time of the Crusades, for the defence of Jerusalem and the protection of pilgrims, founded a House at Hedgerley, long afterwards known as Temple Bulstrode. The land appears to have been given them by Henry de Pinkeni, who at that time held Fulmer manor, and before the end of the twelfth century it had been augmented by grants of land in neighbouring parishes. Richard de Turville gave them 130 acres in Chalfont St. Peter (on which was a water-mill) which came to be known as 'Turvilles land'.

A few years later, land beside the Alderbourne with 'Prestwick' (the 'priests's dwelling') was given to Ankerwyke Priory, from which grew Alderbourne Manor.

In the early years of the next century, many lands in Chalfont St. Peter were given to Missenden Abbey, some by great landowners, some by lesser men, who often took them back at a rent. For example, about 1210, Robert de Braibroc, Sheriff of Beds. and Bucks, granted to the Abbey land he had acquired from Richard de Turville: 'All the land which Thomas de Latier held in Chalfont, and all the land which Robert Kipping held, with Robert himself and his issue, and all the land of the assarts [clearings] in Chalfont which belonged to Richard de Turville.' Here we see afar off 'Newland' (near Shire Lane, the largest and possibly the oldest of the 'new lands' in Chalfont), Layters and Skippings farms, and probably some of the farms near the Oxford Road.

Thus in these years the Abbey was able to build up a 'manor' in Chalfont St. Peter, an estate whose tenants owed varying feudal duties and services to the Abbot. The process did not go unchallenged. In 1229 Henry II's Treasurer, Ranulf de Brito, obtained from the king 'the manor of Chalfont St. Peter'. He probably bought it as a speculation – without knowing or caring very much about the Abbot's rights – with a view to development. He obtained the right to hold an annual fair on July 28 and 29, and a market day every Wednesday. He also set to work with a high hand to bring the whole village under his control. His men invaded 'Mumfords', Ralph de Montfort's farm, took his corn, drove away his beasts, and finally imprisoned Ralph himself (the Abbot's free man). Geoffrey le Stamp had to suffer the loss of his fuel from Stampwell. The Templars' land in Chalfont was also attacked, and their goods distrained. But in 1231 Ranulf Brito was disgraced and banished; the Abbot promptly counter-attacked, and regained all the lands which Richard de Turville had given, together with some houses which Brito had built in the village. All that was left to Brito, when he returned, was 200 acres or so which he had acquired from another de Turville: this is the estate which later emerges as 'Brudenells Manor', centring on 'Chalfont Park'.[5]

In 1229, also, a vicarage was appointed in the Church; and our first vicar was Walter of Aylesbury. Of the Church lands which had been granted to the Abbey, the Abbot retained only two houses; the rest (together with Ranulf Brito's houses in the village) were held as a small manor by the vicar himself.


## THE TEMPLARS AT BULSTRODE

The Templars' House probably stood on or near the site of Moat Farm. (There used to be a lane leading east from that point called Temple Lane.) Little is heard of them, beyond the fact that Henry de Pinkeni (before 1200) had granted them the right to pasture 300 sheep on Fulmer Common; and an Assize case in 1276, when Brother John, the Preceptor, was accused of taking a bribe of half a mark from a certain robber to let him go free. But when, in 1308, the Order was suppressed in England, Edward III seized its very considerable property and goods; and the inventory made then gives an interesting glimpse of their life at Bulstrode. The simple house included a hall, with two tables and trestles, two sleeping tables, and a bell in the rafters; a well-furnished chapel; a kitchen; a cellar (with barrels); a bakehouse, and a workshop, with anvil and hammers. A chaplain, Edmund de Burnham, received for daily services 15¼d. a week, plus an allowance of corn. A useful source of income was that water-mill on 'Turvilles land'. Though their stock was mixed, they evidently specialised in sheep: the inventory includes '100 sheep, 125 mother-sheep, 75 hoggetts, 4 rams and 60 lambs'. The wool was carted to London, and the stock-in-hand included 304 fleeces, 56 lamb-fleeces, 30 lamb-skins, and 44 sheep skins. The staff included 3 carters, a mower, a cowkeeper, 2 shepherds, a swineherd, a ploughman; 16 women were paid for winnowing the corn.[6]

After the disappearance of the Templars, the manor of Temple Bulstrode passed through several hands, until in 1337 it was bestowed upon Bisham Priory (near Marlow) who held it for the next 200 years.


## OKE

Of that detached portion of Iver which is variously called Ake, Oke, Noke and Oak End, we know little in these early years, except that it included a water-mill and a tile-works. The tile-works was probably near the site of 'Chalfont Lodge', which used to be Tilehouse Farm. In 1315 William atte Noke paid a rent of 3s. 4d., 3 quarters of lime, 3,000 common tiles, and 30 ridge-tiles. Tiles were supplied to Windsor Castle in

1353. Traces of the water-mill can still be seen near 'Oak End'. It was acquired in the thirteenth century by a family named de Chaunceaux, and more than 300 years later was still called 'Chauceys Mill alias Noke Mill'.[7]

## UNDER MISSENDEN ABBEY

For more than 350 years, Chalfont St. Peter was linked with Missenden Abbey. This story has been admirably told by Mrs. E. M. Elvey in an article in 'Records of Buckinghamshire' (vol. 17, pt. 2), based upon study of the manor court rolls. You will see from her map (reproduced on the frontispiece) of the fourteenth-century manor, how many of the old names still persist.[8]

According to a rental of 1333, Matthew de la Vache (Chalfont St. Giles) was then the tenant of 'the Feld' and Philips Hill, and John de Asschewelle had 'Ashwells'. At that time Geoffrey de Bulstrode held what we call 'Chalfont Park', and also those lands called 'Turvilles', which had formerly belonged to the Templars (concerning the ownership of which there was a long dispute).[9] John atte Grove ('Grove Park', Narcot Lane) had 'Diddesworth'; Thomas Mareschal, 'Molp' ('Mopes'); and Philip Durdent of Denham held 'Marsham' (which first appears as 'le Maysham' and later as 'Messam') and also a 'Boterfeld' holding ('Butterfield' is a recurring local name). Robert le Mountefort had 'Mumfords', and Sir Ralph de Wedon 'Birchlands' and 'Pitlands', near the Beaconsfield boundary.

'Old Mead', the long narrow strip between the Misbourne and the Amersham Road, formed the precious communal water-meadow. Common Downs, Skolebury, and Old Field were the great Common Fields, in which each tenant had his

15

strip, or strips, separated by 'balks' from his neighbour's land. Soon Latchmoor Common Field ('le Hatch Ryding') was added; and there were other common fields on the other side of the valley, as the name 'Chalfont Common' still recalls.[10]

In the manor-court, held twice a year (sometimes more frequently), tenancies were transferred, fines paid, discipline maintained, and disputes settled. Some of the land was held by men important in the outside world, over whom the Abbot had little control. Some was held by free tenants, who were not slow to maintain their rights. There were, for example, Nicholas le Plomer and his nephew Nicholas, who in 1333 had Layters and Stampwell and other holdings along the Oxford Road (from one of which, that of Gerard de Chalfont, Gerrards Cross probably takes its name). Young Nicholas went hunting and caught hares and partridges in the lord's warren. When he was admonished, his uncle produced a charter granted by an earlier abbot, giving them leave 'to hunt and fish in all the lands, woods, and waters of the Lord Abbot which he has in the vill of Chalfont'. The Plomers, like their neighbour Robert de Montfort, declined to do homage in the Abbot's court, until the Abbot took the case before the King's Justices, who upheld his claim.

Even the villeins, the unfree tenants, though subject to many disabilities, had their rights protected by custom and upheld in the manor court. They were bound to do certain carefully defined services in the lord's fields, to keep their houses in good repair and their land in good heart. But they could sell their land, if they wished, and they could settle it upon their heirs.

A tenant's land might be in a compact block, together with a few strips in one of the common fields, like that of Richard Butterfield who held a house called Redland and 30 acres, with 6 strips in a common field called Denefield; or it might be scattered about in several common fields.

16

The village suffered, like others, from the Black Death in 1346; and here, as elsewhere, after that catastrophe, labour was in short supply and properties fell into decay. Before the end of the century, services owed to the Lord of the Manor were generally commuted into a money-rent. Thus, in 1401, John Boterfeld was admitted to a house and 30 acres 'to be held by him and his, according to the custom of the manor; rendering annually at the Feasts of the Annunciation of the Blessed Mary and of St. Michael 4s. in equal instalments and at Christmas $12\frac{1}{2}$d., reaping the lord's corn for two days with food supplied by the lord, and for two days maintaining himself, carting the lord's corn for one day at his own expense and scything the lord's meadow for one day at his own expense, and haymaking for one day at his own expense, and ploughing the lord's land for two days at his own expense, or he must give the lord 14d. And he will hoe then the lord's land for one day at his own expense. And he shall do the lord's repairs to the extent of 5 wooden stakes, and then have breakfast from the lord. And on the Vigil of St. Thomas the Apostle he shall give one cock. And he shall make suit of court every three weeks and heriot* when it happens. And above this he gives the lord as a fine for entry upon the land 13s. 4d. And he did fealty to the lord, and it is granted by the lord that the said John and his heirs may choose, either to hold the aforesaid lands and tenements in manner or form aforesaid, *or* to pay annually at the Annunciation of the Blessed Mary and of St. Michael 8s. $9\frac{1}{2}$d. instead of the rent and works above mentioned.'

Fifteenth-century Abbots, struggling to keep things going, found themselves up against two powerful men in Chalfont. One of these you may meet in the church. There is a good brass there, of a man in plate-armour and a woman with horned

* Heriot, a fine due on the death of a tenant.

headdress and veil, which commemorates 'William Whappelode, sometime steward of the household of the most reverend Father in God, the most illustrious Lord Henry (Beaufort) Cardinal of England and Bishop of Winchester'. (Another brass commemorates his parents.) William Whappelode acquired the Vache manor at Chalfont St. Giles in 1411, and soon became the most powerful man in the district, representing Bucks. in Parliament, and holding other offices in the County. He held many lands in Chalfont St. Peter and refused to pay rent for them. In his will of 1447 he expressed the wish to be buried 'in a chapel of the Church of St. Peter, before our Lady's altar, where my father and mother are buried'. He also charged his executors – 'as they will answer before the High Judge at the Day of Doom' – to make provision for prayers to be offered for the souls of himself and his wife. This they did by endowing a Chantry in the Church of St. Peter, with rents amounting to £7 per annum from Mumfords and other properties, from which the stipend of a chantry priest was paid.[11]

One of his executors was his friend and neighbour, Edmund Brudenell, of Raans manor in Amersham and 'Brudenells' manor in Chalfont St. Peter. This Edmund's grandson, another Edmund, proved himself an aggressive landlord, buying up all he could, and bullying the Abbot's tenants. For a long time past there had been a trend towards turning over arable land to sheep-farming, which was more profitable; and Edmund evidently decided to cash in on this. He bought the remainder of the lease of the Grange lands, and allowed the house to go to ruins. In one of the earlier attempts of the State to check enclosures (1517) it is recorded that Brudenell had enclosed Layters and Butterfields 'which time out of mind had been ploughed and sown' and also another farm called Hogpittes (near the site of Coldharbour farm). In each case the house had

18

been allowed to fall into decay, and altogether 22 persons had lost their livelihood and been 'driven away in misery'.[12]

Edmund did much to destroy the traditional way of life in the Abbot's manor, which was already crumbling, before, in 1538, Henry VIII decreed the dissolution of the monasteries. In that year Edmund Brudenell died, and his estates in Chalfont St. Peter passed to his daughter, the wife of Robert Drury; and a new era in our history begins.

But before we enter the reign of the Drurys, let us first look at some old houses, take a walk to Horn Hill, and then return to meet some neighbours of the Drurys.

## OLD HOUSES REDISCOVERED

Reminders of those times still occasionally come to light. Hill Farm appeared to be a seventeenth-century house, with considerable later additions. But a thorough examination, in 1967, revealed that the core of the house was a fourteenth-century open hall, with timbers still blackened from the open fire in the centre. In the following century, the master, or his dame, wanting more spacious private accommodation, had added a wing of two full storeys; and late in the seventeenth century the old hall had been divided, and a floor inserted. The original hall had an open cruck truss, rarely found in this region; and the many alterations and conditions had left in one building the whole story of roof construction.

An even more striking example of what may lie behind a nineteenth-century mask was discovered when houses opposite the church were demolished in 1966 to make room for redevelopment. One, which had been divided, was found to be a substantial fifteenth-century timber-framed house, with open hall and wings, having crown post roof-trusses and a splendid stone fireplace.[12a]

The big house in 'Chalfont Park', long known as 'The Old House', was a house of great importance in the life of the village – perhaps the house in which Edmund Brudenell and Robert Drury lived. During alterations there in 1966 a wall and doorway of a fifteenth or sixteenth century house were discovered on the south side.


## HORN HILL

There is a farm at West Hide (in the parish of Rickmansworth) called Linsters. This was once the centre of a small manor, which included most of the farms and houses of Horn Hill, and lands in Chalfont St. Peter. It was held in the fifteenth century by members of the Lynster family, but by 1520 had passed to the hospital of the Savoy. When, soon after this, the lands of the Savoy came to the Crown, King Edward VI, in 1553, 'considering and pondering upon the scandalous and wretched condition of the poor, sick and infirm men now lying begging in the public places and ways of the City of London to their no slight grievance and pain', gave to St. Thomas's Hospital the Manor of Linsters, West Hide. Horn Hill, one of the most ancient, remains one of the most charming portions of the parish of Chalfont St. Peter, but it has an intricate history of its own, as most of its houses stood in Hertfordshire.[13]


## THE LEGEND OF BULSTRODE

One of the most distinguished members of the family of Bulstrode was Sir Richard, who died in 1711, at the age of 101.

In the following year a volume of his letters was published, and in the preface is this story:

'When William the Conqueror had subdued this Kingdom to his Obedience, he granted the Estate of the Shobbingtons, whose capital Seat, now likewise called Bulstrodes, was situated in the middle of a fine park by Gerards Cross near Beaconsfield, and had been in their Family for several ages before, to a certain Norman lord who had come over to him: of which the Shobbington, who then enjoyed it, having notice, he resolved rather to die upon the Spot, than tamely to suffer himself to be turned out of Possession of that Inheritance, which had descended to him from his Ancestors. In this Resolution he armed his Servants and his Tenants, whose Number was very considerable. Upon which the Norman Lord, who had advice of it, obtained of the King a thousand of his Regular Troops, to help him to take Possession of the Estate by Force, whereupon Shobbington applied himself to his Relations and Neighbours to assist him: and the two ancient Families of the Hampdens and Penns took Arms, together with their Servants and Tenants, and came to his Relief. When they were all joined, they cast up Works, whose Remains appear to this Day, in the Place where the Park now is; and the Norman Lord, with his Forces, came and encamped before their Intrenchments. Now whether that they wanted Horses, or not is uncertain, but the Story goes, That having managed a parcel of Bulls, they mounted them and sallying out of their Intrenchments in the night, surprised the Normans in their Camp, killed many of them, and put the Rest to Flight. The King having Intelligence of it and not thinking it safe for him, while his Power was yet new and unsettled, to drive a daring and obstinate People to despair, sent a Herald to them: to know what they would have, and promised Shobbington a Safe Conduct, if he would come to court; which Shobbington accordingly did, riding thither upon a Bull. Being introduced into the Royal Presence, the King asked him his Demands, and why he alone dared to resist, when the rest of the Kingdom had submitted to his Government, and owned him for their Sovereign? Shobbington answered, That he and his Ancestors had long been inhabitants of this Island, and had enjoyed that Estate for many years; that if the King would permit him to keep it, he would become his Subject, and be faithful to him, as he had been to his Predecessors. The King gave him his Royal Word, that he would, and immediately granted him the Free Enjoyment of his Estate. Upon which the Family was from hence called Shobbington, alias Bulstrode, but in Process of time the first Name was discontinued, and that of Bulstrode only has remained to them. The Truth of this Story is not only confirmed by long Traditions in the Family, but by several Memoirs which they have still remaining, and by the Ruins of the Works, that are to this Day seen in the Park of Bulstrodes, as well as by the Crest of their Arms, which is a Bull's Head Cabossed Gules.'

One wonders what lies behind this splendid story. Perhaps some legend of an heroic exploit: more certainly, some family connection with the village of Shabbington (near Thame). It may well be that there were Bulstrodes on that hill where 'Bulstrode' now is before the Conqueror came: for the name appears in these parts early in the twelfth century. There they long continued, a line of minor gentry, in their small manor which is generally called 'Hedgerley Bulstrode' to distinguish it from 'Temple Bulstrode'.

Hedgerley Bulstrode was until the nineteenth century in a curious detached portion of Upton: and the family owned other lands at Upton, Chalvey, and Horton.[14] Richard, who died in 1503, was Keeper of the Wardrobe to Henry VII's Queen Margaret: Edward, his son, Squire of the Body to

22

Henry VII and Henry VIII. Edward married three times: a brass in Upton Church represents him with wife No. 1 and 4 sons, and wife No. 2 with 6 sons and 2 daughters: a brass in Hedgerley Church commemorates his third wife and her 10 children.[15]

Robert Drury served on various county commissions with George Bulstrode and his son Thomas. Thomas died in 1560, and his will is worth recalling. He describes himself as 'Thomas Bulstred of Hedgerley Bulstred in the Parish of Upton, esquire'. His confession of faith is stoutly Protestant (three Protestants had been burnt at the stake in Uxbridge three years earlier). He quotes, from the Genevan version, *Job* c. 19 vv 25–27 ('I know that my Redeemer liveth . . .') and hopes that his bestowal of his goods may be accepted as 'fruit of faith': 'I do not suppose my merit be by good bestowing of them, but my merit is the faith of Jesus Christ only'. 'A godly sermon' is to be preached at his burial 'by some godly and well-learned man not under the degree of Master of Arts'; another, when the month is up: and another, when the year is up. He leaves to his son Francis his manor in Horton, his long-bow, the quiver of shafts and arrows, a corselet and a pike: and to his son Edward, all his books, his poll-axe, daggers, sword, and cross-bow, and a quiver of arrows and bolts. After other bequests to relatives, servants, and the poor, he leaves the residue to his wife Ann: 'She shall have my house at Hedgerley as I did use to occupy it, and my farm at Coltnet (Horton), to keep these houses in good repair, and not to let them, except to a son.'[16]

Thomas was succeeded by his son Edward. This Edward was the grandfather of the Richard mentioned above, who became Ambassador at Brussels, and died at the age of 101. One of Edward's daughters married Sir James Whitelocke, and became the mother of Bulstrode Whitelocke, historian of the Commonwealth; another, Cicely, a court beauty of wit and

23

high character, was celebrated in verse both by Ben Jonson and by John Donne.[17]

But to return to the Drurys, and to the time of Henry VIII.


## THE DRURYS

The Drurys were an East Anglian family.[18] Sir Robert, a barrister who was elected Speaker of the House of Commons in 1495, had two sons – William, who carried on the line at Hawsted in Suffolk, and Robert, who married Elizabeth Brudenell and settled in Chalfont, leasing lands from the last Abbot of Missenden. When Elizabeth's father died, Robert Drury came into possession of the manors of Brudenells and Hedgerley in his wife's right. In the same year (1538) he bought, for £142, the Temple Bulstrode manor. Two years later, after the dissolution of the Monasteries, he acquired the Abbot's manor in Chalfont St. Peter, with pieces in Chalfont St. Giles and Iver. Soon afterwards he bought both Turvilles lands and the Chantry lands. He was now monarch of almost all he surveyed, and for the first time all our manors (except Hedgerley Bulstrode) were brought together under one ownership.

He was evidently a capable man, and a just man: and Chalfont St. Peter benefited from his strong rule. A new life comes into the court-rolls. Some, at least, of those who had long ignored the Abbot were brought to heel. Houses were rebuilt, order restored in the common fields, encroachments checked, hedges and balks reinstated, ditches cleared, pigs ringed, and the village pound repaired. Old customs were summarized: strays are to be proclaimed in church and market place; poaching is punished, whether in woods, warren or stream, but a common net to catch choughs, crows and rooks is allowed as of

24

old. Constables and ale-tasters are appointed. John Fox the baker is fined for selling bread without licence, and William Bocher the butcher, for overcharging.

Sir Robert Drury was three times Sheriff of Bucks. – he was knighted on the first occasion, in 1546 – a loyal supporter of King Henry VIII, who served on various county commissions. The parish register records the burial in 1577 of 'that venerable man, Robert Drury, knight, Lord of the Manor and Patron of this Church', and there is elsewhere a record of his tomb which stood in the chancel.[19] One of his sons, Sir William, was Marshal of Berwick and Lord Chief Justice of Ireland, in the time of Elizabeth I (there is a portrait of him in the National Portrait Gallery). Another, Sir Dru, was one of the warders of Mary, Queen of Scots, at Fotheringay, and afterwards Constable of the Tower. Sir Robert's manors and lands in Norfolk, Suffolk, Essex and Bucks. were divided amongst his children: and his estates in these parts were inherited by his son Robert.

There are memorials in the church to this Robert (died 1592) and his son Sir Henry Drury (d. 1617). Henry was one of five Drury cousins knighted by James I before his coronation. Drury Lane in London takes its name from the family's town house. 'Drury House' was let for some time to Shakespeare's friend and patron, the Earl of Southampton, and it was there that Essex's rebellion was planned.[20] So we may imagine Sir Henry in the midst of that exciting London of Shakespeare's later years. His affairs in Chalfont St. Peter were capably managed, he added to his estates, and when he died left to his son William, then aged 20, extensive lands in these parishes, as well as a manor in Norfolk, and 'the Drury House and other houses in Drury Lane, in the parish of St. Clement Danes'.

But the first part of the seventeenth century was a particularly difficult time for the country gentry, and William was soon obliged to mortgage some parts of his estate and to sell

25

others. (It may be that, like some other members of the Drury family, he also suffered as a Papist.) Even his mother's manor of Temple Bulstrode, which Sir Henry had settled on her when they married, was much diminished; and she retired to live with her daughter, Mrs. John Penn, of Penn, where her memorial may be seen in the Church. We catch one further glimpse of William Drury when, in 1641, 'blind, lame, and destitute of estate', he made a pathetic appeal to the House of Lords against a mortgagee who had taken possession of Hedgerley Manor.[21]

He had sold in 1626 nearly all he had in Chalfont St. Peter and Hedgerley. The deed of sale, which marks the break-up of the estate, provides much interesting information about Chalfont St. Peter at that time. 'William Drury of Hedgerley Esq' sells to 'Henry Bulstrode of Horton Esq' for £13,900, the manor of Chalfont St. Peter, with the rectory, parsonage, tithes and advowson of the church; the manor of Brudenells, the Chantry of Whaplode, all the houses and lands called Mason (Marsham) End, Turvilles lands, the water-mill called Noke Mill etc. – except for certain leases specified. From these we learn that Thomas Baldwin has 'the Ould Place' at £150 p.a. (i.e. the old Brudenells manor house in 'Chalfont Park'), Mopes (4d) and Stampwell (£24); John Russell has Chalfont Lodge Farm, called the Tilehouse (£60); Richard Playter has Noke Mill, with lands and waters, at the substantial rent of £94 p.a.; the Playter family had also Bidwell's Wood, adjoining Mill Lane, and Gallows Wood beyond it; Robert Duck has the Grange, where his rent is £25, plus 1 qr. wheat, 1 qr. barley, 1 qr. oats, and entertainment for two days and one night twice yearly, for the lord and his retinue to keep court; Richard Whitchurch has Mumfords (£40), Thomas Tredway a farm called Butterfield's End, with 40 acres of Siblets Wood, and Richard Baker has both Dorsetts ('Marsham Farm') and a larger farm called Hatches (probably 'Latchmoor'). Robert Tibby rents the Greyhound, with 14 acres, for £22, and Thomas Franklin the Swan at £13 6s. 8d. Richard Kirby has a blacksmith's shop (on Gold Hill) for which he pays £2 10s. 0d. and Robert Randall, a labourer, a cottage for which he must render each year three woodcocks.[22]

Some of the sixteenth and seventeenth century houses remain, notably Mumfords, Layters Farm, Hollytree Farm,[23] Waterhall, Ashwells, Mopes and Hill Farm: others have been pulled down within living memory. The picture on page viii shows some sixteenth and seventeenth century cottages near the church which were pulled down in 1933. It also shows (on the right, where the shopping centre now is) a larger seventeenth-century house, which stood in front of what used to be called 'Barrack Yard', into which a high covered gateway led. This interesting house was examined by Mr. Clive Rouse in 1938 (when it was in process of demolition) who found there a complete scheme of mural paintings. (Amateur painters and house-decorators, please note!) There were several illuminated texts, a lively representation of David and Goliath, and a spirited painting of a unicorn. It was James I who introduced the Scottish unicorn into our Royal Arms, and this with the charming rose-and-thistle design found on the opposite wall, suggests that the owner was celebrating the Union of the English and Scottish Crowns in 1603.[24]

## INNS

Whether his house was originally an inn or not, we know that in 1683 it was the Crossed Keys Inn, occupied by Tobias Goodridge at an annual rent of 2s. 6d. and taking its name, no doubt, from St. Peter's crossed keys; which brings us to the

27

subject of inns. You noticed the 'Greyhound' and the 'Swan' in that deed of 1626. A list compiled in 1577 of innkeepers and alehouse keepers in Bucks. gives the names of William ffrancklyn and William Noble, innkeepers in Chalfont St. Peter, and Richard Smythe, Ayleshouse-keeper. William Franklin probably had the Swan; William Noble possibly the Greyhound.[25]

The Greyhound still stands: the Swan was opposite – only the barn remains, now ingeniously converted to the uses of the Youth Club. The Swan, of course, is the Bucks. emblem: the Greyhound was the Drury crest, so perhaps the 'Greyhound' originated with them. Richard Smith had the 'Bell' near the site of the present 'White Hart'. A 'Catalogue of the Taverns in Tenne Shires about London', published in 1636, mentions a tavern at 'Chaffant' kept by Robert Ducke. This was the 'Lion' – Lion Yard was a little above Joiners Lane. In 1683 we hear also of 'the Starr Inn' and 'the Five Bells', which, like the Crossed Keys and the Red Lion, were part of the manor of the Vicarage.[26]

At Gerrards Cross, the earliest inn of which we have clear evidence is 'The Goat' (later the White Hart) which is mentioned in 1645, and stood a little west of the 'Bull'; but there was probably also an inn or ale-house where the 'French Horn' now stands. The Oxford Road was a dangerous road then (as it is still). In December 1691 'a waggon laden with their Majestyes' money was assaulted by several Theives and Robbed', Joseph Perkyns, ostler 'at the Oxford Arms Inn at Gerrards Cross', 'goeing with Armes to defend it', was seriously wounded. He applied to the Justices for help in paying his doctor's bill, which they granted. The 'Oxford Arms' was evidently a predecessor of the 'Bull'.

In the following year Sir Roger Hill, of Denham Place, entered in his Justice's diary: 'Hue & Cry upon a robbery said to be committed last night neer Gerrards Cross heath upon Robert Lord of Little Tue, Com. Oxon. yeoman, by 2 men, one a young man in a brown wig on a bay horse with a sprig tayle, ye other a short thick man on foot, both in blewish cloths, he swore he lost about 20s. in silver, a pair of lead colored stokins, a sad cloured cloth riding coate severall neck cloths & handkerchifes & his silver sleeve buttons and his horse, being a bay with a blase in his face, the neer foot being white, 15 hands high.'[27]

## ST. PETER'S

Church and inn often went together in village life; and it is high time we looked at the church and its vicars. The church was not that which we see now, but an earlier building, which had already been altered and enlarged during the centuries, and evidently had two altars. When extensive repairs became necessary in 1965, many fragments of moulded stone of various periods, and of medieval timbers, were found, and the foundations of the earlier building were revealed.[28]

In the reign of Edward VI, careful enquiry was made concerning the goods of the churches (many of which were later seized by the Crown). In 1552, the Commissioners (Sir Robert Drury and others) agreed with the Churchwardens of St. Peter's, William Duck and Richard Taylor, an inventory of that Church's possessions. It is quite an impressive list, including three silver chalices with patens, two corporas (for carrying the reserved Sacrament), nine vestments (one 'of green velvet figured with daisies and birds'), four copes (one 'of blue bawdkyn with orfreys of nedill-worke') two copper-and-gilt crosses, two censers of latten, 'with a shippe', a pair of latten candlesticks for the high altar, 'one pair of organs', 'five bells

in a ring' and 'one other litell bell commonly called the sanctus'.
Whaplode's chantry had already been dissolved, and there remained 'no implements belonging to the said Chantry, but only
one vestment for the priest to sing mass in, which is priced at
13s. 4d. and remaineth in the hands of Thomas Langshaw', the
last chantry priest.[29]

Of the earlier vicars, most are little more than names to us
(there is a list of them in the church), but occasionally we catch
a glimpse of one, in the fields, in his manor court, or in the
church. Remember that the vicar had considerable lands to
farm; and one, at least, of them – John Bryan – took on also
other lands. Probably they needed to, for the living was far
from a fat one. According to a schedule of 1529, Francis
Pollard the vicar, received £5 a year; Robert Semer, his curate,
£6: and Thomas Langshaw, the chantry priest, £6. A brass
representing a priest in mass vestments commemorates Robert
Hanson, who was the vicar at the time the Abbey came to an
end, and also Vicar of Little Missenden. It would seem that he
was a Yorkshireman, for in his will he remembered the
Churches of Duffield and Holmfirth, near Huddersfield, as well
as the churches and the poor of Chalfont St. Peter and
Missenden. (He also, by the way, bequeathed to a cousin at
Oxford 'a standing rote' – a kind of lyre.)[30]

These were difficult times for Churchmen, who were required to acknowledge, as Head of the Church, the Pope,
imperious Henry, Protestant Edward, Catholic Mary, and
middle-of-the-road Elizabeth, all within the space of one
generation. Hanson's predecessor Roger Edgeworth, for his
anti-Protestant sentiments, gained rapid preferment, and became Chancellor of Bath and Wells; Hanson's successor,
Thomas Slitherst, the first President of Trinity College, Oxford,
for his anti-Protestant sentiments, was deprived of his living.[31]

Queen Elizabeth wanted to know not only that the church

services were being observed with due order, but also that the church was playing its important part in the urgent task of poor relief. Thus our churchwardens of 1601 report: 'It may please you to understand by these present that our neighbours do in reasonable good sort repair to the church, and further we have given a stock of corn to the use of the poor which cometh to the sum of £20 and upwards, and withal there is a second supply for the relief of the poor which cometh to the sum 9s by the week, which is weekly to be distributed.'

The vicarage, next to the church, was already a sizeable house, consisting of 'five bays built of timber and covered with tiles', with hall, kitchen, parlour, and seven rooms above, and several outhouses and barns, some tiled, some thatched, a little garden next to the churchyard and a glebe meadow with some fruit trees. The other glebe lands were the fields running westwards from the church between the parish boundary and Common Down, three fields called Goldhill Closes (behind the site of 'Rock House') and some pieces in the common fields – in all about 60 acres.[32]


## FULMER AND ITS NEW CHURCH

Here let us look across the border and salute Fulmer Church and its builder. Fulmer manor, which for much of its long history had belonged to the owner of Stoke Poges, had been granted in 1606, 'for service of one rose', to Sir Marmaduke Darrell. Marmaduke Darrell was for more than forty years Victualler to the Navy, responsible for supplying not only food and drink but many things beside. He was well acquainted with Drake and Hawkins and the other sea-captains of the time, and a member of the Council which planned the expedition against Spain. He was with the Fleet at Plymouth on a memorable day in July 1588, when he and the mayor, looking out, saw on the horizon the Spanish galleons approaching, and was able to send a message to the Queen that Lord Howard had led out the English Fleet to engage the Armada.

The latter part of his long life saw a phenomenal rise in the demand for coal in and around London; and Sir Marmaduke, with two or three of his colleagues, secured the contract for carrying coals from Newcastle, with a royalty of 12d. on every chaldron.

This was the distinguished Civil Servant who had come to live at Fulmer. He built a new manor house there, on the beautiful site now occupied by Fulmer Place, acquired other properties in the neighbourhood, and showed himself a generous patron to the village.

Old Fulmer Church, nearly a mile further up the valley, was in a sad state of disrepair, and the villagers found the path to it very miry: and so Sir Marmaduke Darell, the lord of the manor, gave them a new church. It was consecrated on All Saints Day 1610, and it contains a fine memorial to Sir Marmaduke and his family, with an inscription relating that he was Victualler to the Navy in the days of the first Queen Elizabeth, and Cofferer (Paymaster) to James I and Charles I, and 'was favoured by all these renowned princes and employed in matters of great trust for the space of fifty years, in all which he acquitted himself with credit and commendation'. There are few English churches of this period, and St. James, Fulmer, is certainly a beautiful example.[33]

## PURITANS AND LAUDIANS

But now the battle is mounting between High Church and Puritan, mingled with the battle between King and Parliament. James Bradshaw, who was vicar in 1626, when Henry Bul-

32

strode bought the living, was a Laudian. 'Laudian' we must say now, for already the most powerful force in the bench of bishops is William Laud, pious, industrious, and ruthless, soon to become Archbishop of Canterbury. Laud set himself to enforce decent and uniform standards in doctrines, services and buildings. A thorough enquiry made in 1637 revealed the deplorable condition of many of the church buildings. (It gives us, by the way, one of our very few glimpses of the private chapel at Hedgerley Bulstrode: 'There is a loft round about it above, to look into it through the lattice casements.' St. Peter's Church fares better than some others: evidently something had been done since it was reported in 1612 that one side was 'so broken that a hog may creep through'. In 1637, there are still some holes – in the steeple. Inside the church are some high family pews that will have to be cut down (a very common complaint). The rood-loft door behind the pulpit is 'to be stopt up handsomely', and the Communion table needs improvement. Two flagons, a new chalice, and a poor man's box, are to be provided. The register, we are told, dates from 28 March 1538.[34]

But dilapidated buildings were not Laud's major problem: he had also to deal with refractory parsons and people. Bucks. since the days of the Lollards had been noted for nonconformity, and at this time had many Puritan ministers and gentry, including the influential John Hampden. Laud had a loyal supporter in Dr. John Andrewes, the Rector of Beaconsfield, who writes to the Archbishop:

'They keep up their brabblings and janglings in our church about election of officers, and their accounts, and every base matter: yea, and keep their musters, or inspection of arms, in our churchyard. Many gad from church to church on Sundays to hear Puritanical sermons in other churches, contrary to the law. Few or none come to Church on Holy Days in all the year, not even the churchwardens. Many sit at divine service with their hats on, and some lie along the pews, their heads covered, even at the Litany or the Ten Commandments.'

It was decided to make an example of some of the Puritan parsons, and the Archbishop's Commissioner, when he held his Visitation at Amersham in 1635, suspended from office the Rev. Elkanah Gladman of Chesham, and the Rev. Thomas Valentine of Chalfont St. Giles.

On Christmas Day that year there was a scandalous affair at Fulmer. Gervase Good, the constable of Chalfont St. Peter, was alleged to have arrested someone for debt in the church, in the course of the Communion Service. Dr. Andrewes, reporting, seizes the occasion to express once more his concerns. Gervase Good denied that he had arrested the man in Church: he 'only whispered him in the ear, and carried him to Gerrards Cross, and there did arrest him'. But others told a different tale, and Dr. Andrewes concludes that Good was at fault: but adds that it may be said in extenuation that 'the people hereabouts had been so mistaught that they did not think Sunday, or even Christmas Day, more sacred that any other day, or the Church a place of greater holiness or respect than stables or barns'. 'In the meantime give me leave to tell you that you yourself are banned and cursed to the pit of hell for suspending Mr. Valentine of St. Giles Chalfont and Mr. Gladman . . . Or thus (as I hear) the women talk up and down these parts. The men put in their horns and their tongues too.'[35]

The men did not all restrain their tongues. One Isaac Penington had come to live at Chalfont St. Peter at the Grange. Much of the history of Chalfont St. Peter might be written around the story of the Grange (now the Holy Cross Convent). Through all the years that Missenden Abbey held the manor, the Grange was its 'Manor house' in Chalfont St. Peter, where the Abbot's court was held, and the Abbot's bailiff lived. In Edmund Brudenell's time (as we have seen) it was allowed to fall into a sad state of disrepair, but the Drurys had evidently put it into better shape, and now, in 1637, Henry Bulstrode had sold it, and extensive lands with it, to a relative by marriage, 'Isaac Penington of London esq.'[36]

Penington was a remarkable man, one of the key figures in the turbulent history of that time, when both King and Parliament were bidding for the support of the City of London. An out-and-out Parliament man, as a substantial citizen, a leading alderman (Lord Mayor in 1642) and one of the City's representatives in the Long Parliament, he was a living and fiery link between the Puritans in Parliament, in the City government, and amongst the citizens at large. A sincerely religious man, he served as a vestry-man in the famous Puritan church of St. Stephen's, Coleman Street, and was well acquainted with all the Puritan leaders, and an implacable opponent of the policies of Archbishop Laud.[37]

This was the gentleman who had taken the Grange as a country house. He did not find his parish church congenial. One of his complaints was that there was no Sunday afternoon 'lecture'; and when the vicar, Mr. Bradshaw, replied that the Archbishop had forbidden such lectures, Penington had some plain words to say about the Archbishop. He also had a gardener, after his own heart, who did not scruple to argue theology with his Vicar.

Poor Mr. Bradshaw! Laud's power was waning: and our vicar chose this unfortunate moment to utter some of his most extravagant remarks, declaring that 'the bishops' courts were the suburbs of heaven, and their officers the very supremacies next to archangels: and that to refuse to appear before them, or to use any but the Book of Common Prayer, or to preach

35

twice on a Sunday, were all damnable sins'.[38] He was soon afterwards deprived of his living, by order of the House of Commons, and the Rev. Thomas Holl came to be our vicar in his stead – of whom more later.[39]


## ROUNDHEADS AND CAVALIERS

Mr. Holl came to us about the time of the beginning of the Civil War, that unhappy conflict that caused much misery and divided many families. We were mostly Roundheads. Henry Bulstrode was appointed to raise the Trained Bands throughout the Chiltern Hundred, with Henry Gould of Oak End as one of his lieutenants, and young George Fleetwood of the Vache raised a troop of horse; and we may be sure that some of our men went with them. Troops and rumours travelled along the high road, between the King's headquarters at Oxford, and Parliament's H.Q. in London: High Wycombe was a kind of frontier town, and Beaconsfield a rallying point for the Parliament forces. In November 1642 came 'joyful news' of the victory of the parliamentary forces over Prince Rupert near Aylesbury; and in the following August, Essex himself rode through 'Chaffant' at the head of 7,000 men, making a wide detour round Oxford, on his way to the relief of Gloucester. 'On March 23, 1643, the Earl Carnarvon and Prince Rupert with other great ones, marched to Wendover and plundered all the towns thereabouts.' But we saw little of the actual fighting, and for the most part, we just carried on, grumbling because we were short-handed, because horses and wagons and stocks had been commandeered, and because taxes were heavy, for wars cost money. At last came news of the crowning victory of Worcester, and we saw Cromwell himself pass through, on his way to Westminster, driving a horde of Scottish prisoners before him.[40]

In Commonwealth times, great changes in Church and State were made – on paper: how far they affected the lives of ordinary folk varied from place to place. One regulation which was much resented discouraged marriages in church; and indeed, our parish register records few marriages in this period. Parliament did, at least, increase our vicar's stipend by £33 a year. Mr. Holl remained our vicar from 1643 to 1679, contriving not to be turned out by either party, keeping the respect of his people, and dying, as he lived, a poor man. His son Richard became a shoemaker in Chesham, and it is pleasant to find that, not long before he died in 1679, the old man was able to baptize his great-grandson there.[41]

## EARLY QUAKERS

How did Mr. Holl cope, one wonders, with some very non-conforming Non-conformists in his parish? In 1654 Alderman Penington's son, another Isaac Penington, had married a well-to-do widow, Lady Mary Springett, and they had come to live at the Grange, with her daughter Gulielma. Much against his father's wishes, Isaac and his wife had turned Quakers, and their house soon became a meeting-place for Friends from far and near. George Fox himself was there in 1658, about the time of Cromwell's death: and there young Thomas Ellwood came to visit them, and at a Meeting at the Grove first saw the Light. Thereafter he was a frequent visitor, and eventually stayed as tutor to the Penington children. The Quakers were always in trouble; they did not attend their parish church, nor pay tithes, nor doff their hats, and they would not take an oath; when all 'conventicles' were forbidden, they continued to meet

37

for worship. In consequence, many of them spent years in and out of filthy seventeenth-century prisons. Isaac Penington spent several periods in Aylesbury jail, generally in the company of such other local stalwarts as George Salter and Henry Tredway of Hedgerley, and William Russell of Jordans Farm.

Ellwood, in his admirable autobiography, tells how he brought a visitor to the Grange – a middle-aged Independent named John Okey – on a day in 1661, when it happened that leading Friends from other parts of the country were present. On the Sunday morning, they were gathered in their silent Meeting, when suddenly they heard the clatter of horses, and a party of soldiers rode up to the house. 'We all sat still in our place, except John Okey, who sat next to me. But he, being of a profession that approved Peter's advice to his Lord "to save himself" soon took the alarm, and with the nimbleness of a stripling, cutting a caper over a form that stood before him, ran quickly out at a private door, which led through the parlour into the gardens, and thence into an orchard, where he hid himself in a place so secure, and withal so convenient for his intelligence by observation of what passed, that no one of the family could have found a likelier.'

Meanwhile, the soldiers tramped in. The officer in charge was civil enough, but his orders were to break up the meeting, and to take the leaders before a magistrate. So to Denham Court they trudged, to appear before Sir William Bowyer. Sir William examined them, and decided he must commit them to prison; but each time his clerk drafted a mittimus, the Friends found some flaw in it. At length, the exasperated magistrate sent them home, telling them they would hear from him in the morning. Returning to the Grange, they found Mary Penington and the other Friends still sitting in the meeting, and amongst them a very shame-faced John Okey.

Another story Ellwood tells is of a Quaker funeral procession at Amersham, which was rudely interrupted by an important-looking gentleman, who rushed out of an inn, sword in hand. This was Ambrose Bennett esq. of Hedgerley Bulstrode, a magistrate. He laid about him with the flat of his sword, sent the coffin tumbling to the ground, and ordered the constables to arrest these men. When another magistrate had been found – Sir Thomas Clayton of the Vache – the Quakers were once more committed to Aylesbury gaol.

It was in Penington's fourth spell in prison that a heavy blow fell on the family. Old Alderman Penington, who had been one of Charles I's judges, had been imprisoned in the Tower (where he died) and all his estates confiscated, and now the younger Isaac and his family were evicted from the Grange. They found refuge for a time at Bottrells farm, Chalfont St. Giles, and afterwards at Bury farm, Amersham.

But the rest of these things – how in the Plague Year, Thomas Ellwood found a cottage at Chalfont St. Giles for his blind friend and tutor, John Milton, how William Penn took Gulielma Springett in marriage at King's farm, Chorleywood, how in 1688 Jordan's Meeting House was built (with William Grimsdale of Maltman's Green as one of its trustees) – these things have been told elsewhere – and we must leave them, with a special salute to those indomitable ladies, Mary Penington and Gulielma Penn, and a remembrance of our other local stalwarts. When the Archdeacon carried out his Visitation in 1662, nine persons in Chalfont St. Peter were reported for non-attendance at church. Besides Isaac Penington and his wife, they were George and Rebecca Salter, Edward Barton and his wife, John Monk, Mary, wife of Henry Watkins (of the Red Lion) and the wife of William Grassingham. All (except Monk) are identifiable as Quakers.[42]

# TWO SILVER SPOONS

Some of the men and women of those days we catch sight of for a moment when they appear in a court of law – or when they write their wills, wills that take us back to times when possessions were few and precious. Thomas Butterfield, yeoman, bequeathes to his daughter Marie 'the two silver spoons given to my first wife on her marriage day', and to his two sons 'six dozen silver buttons'. Richard Playtor of Noke Mill, miller, leaves to his granddaughter Elizabeth 'a cubbard standing in my bed chamber, and her grandmother's gowne'. Thomas Wetherley, of Tubbs farm, bequeathes to his wife, besides their bed and other household goods, 'one brown cow, and one hogge of bacon which is in the chimney'. John Monk, husbandman, leaves each of his grandchildren a lamb. Neighbourly Sibbell Cawdry, widow, leaves 'a pair of sheets apiece to Goodwife Craft and Goodwife Nashe, one sheet each to Widow Charsley and Widow Batchelor', and 10s. 'to the poor that dwell at this end of the town'. Gervase Good ('Jarvis Goade' it is spelt) – whom we met earlier, creating a disturbance in Fulmer church – remembers all his children, but had evidently a special fondness for his youngest, Frances, who is to have 'three pewter dishes, the best coverlet, a blanket, my flock-bed, one joyned bedstead, one feather bolster, one feather pillow, a pillow-beere, one brass porridge-pot, one high joyned stool, a boulting-tub, a corne-tub, two pairs of sheets, two table napkins, one diaper napkin', and £8 when she reaches the age of 18. 'And whereas William Eastwood the elder, of Chalfont, did out of his good-will offer to be at the charge of one barrel of beer at my burial, I give to the said William my best green suit, my doublet and hose, my short coat and green stockings, my garters and girdle, and my best hat.'[43]

# THE CHURCH HOUSE AFFAIR

Others we may meet on the occasion of a village row. The manor of Chalfont St. Peter had been bought in 1650 by a prosperous local farmer, Richard Whitchurch, of Mumfords (and Mumfords remained the 'Manor House' for 300 years.)[44] He does not seem to have been very popular in the village. Near the church stood an old building called the Church House, which the villagers had always thought of as belonging to the parish. In days gone by, they had had their Whitsun and Midsummer Ales there, junketings at which a good time was had by all, and a little money raised for the Church. Now Richard Whitchurch has let it, at £3 a year, to a young butcher, John Copland, who has his shop there, and his slaughter-house behind, next to the church. The villagers protested, and at an enquiry held at Amersham in September 1665, a verdict was given in their favour: Richard Whitchurch is to pay over £20 of rent, release and quitclaim the premises to the Vicar and churchwardens, and pay costs. But Richard appealed, and a further enquiry was held in the following August at the Red Lion in Chalfont St. Peter, kept by Joseph Freer.

The oldest inhabitant is brought out – Eldred Newman, said to be 'about a hundred years old'. But he maintained that it was the lord of the manor who had had the letting of the house in the past, and had repaired it; and added that Church Ales had been discontinued 'by reason of the disorders that usually fell out after them'. John Newman, yeoman, aged 60, remembered that when he and three other young men wanted to keep a Midsummer Ale, they gave the churchwardens 20s. to have it in the Church House. Winloe Grimsdell of 'Hugerley', added that the lord used to contribute a bushel of wheat and an angel in money. Thomas Egleton, 36, husbandman, remembered that a school used to be kept in the House, and that sometimes poor people were allowed to occupy part of it. John Monk, weaver, aged 39, said that his father used to live there, as Mr William Drury said he might, provided he paid no rent: he used to give the churchwardens 4s. a year to keep the church clock in repair. Since then 'an ancient woman' had occupied it, but she had now been removed to an almshouse. But John Well, husband-man, maintained that poor people had been obliged to leave it, because they could not 'lye dry'. And John Aldridge and Ralph Cock, bricklayers and carpenters, gave evidence that they had repaired it at Mr. Whitchurch's expense, which cost him £18. However, Robert Dell, aged 54, parish clerk, produced the ancient parish books, as kept by his father, who had been parish clerk before him: and the records and figures seem to have carried most weight with the jurors. The Vicar and church-wardens appear to have won in the end, for a few years later 'Two Church Houses' are mentioned amongst their posses-sions.[45]

## ENTER ST. JOHN'S COLLEGE

The King had come home, and most Englishmen were glad of it. The Restoration Year was marked by one event which has had lasting influence upon our village life. Sir Thomas Allen of Finchley had bought the living of the church in 1645 from Colonel Thomas Bulstrode, and in 1660, grateful for the King's return, and grateful to his old College, he gave it to St. John's College, Oxford, who have ever since presented the Vicars of St. Peter's. The College has two rather charming notes from the good man. The first is in acknowledgement of their letter of thanks:

'I heartily thank you and your society for your gracious

42

acceptance of my love. Mr. Holl, the vicar, shall send you the
£20 due . . . The living yielded £60 this year, I am informed:
but sometimes the fall of timber doth much better it. I should
be better satisfied if it were more proportionate to my desires
and your merit. But the Lord be Praised that gave it to me to
give it unto you. So presenting my service to your much-
honoured self and college, I rest, your servant, Thomas Allen.'

The other relates to some arrears of tithes:

'Your under-tenant at Chalfont St. Peter wants authority to
sue some for arrears of tithes. He must do it now in the name
of the College. They were never sued yet: but I know their
constitution so well, that I assure you a little bit of green wax
will do more with them than 104 sermons from the Vicar
yearly . . . The Lord preserve you and yours here and eternally.
So prayeth, Sir, your true friend and servant, Thos. Allen.'[46]


## MR. DUDLEY REWSE

The King had come home; and there were jobs to be had.
Mr. Dudley Rewse, who had acquired Brudenells Manor, and
was on good terms with the Darrells of Fulmer and the Palmers
of Dorney, in 1665 secured the post of bailiff and paymaster
of Windsor Castle (the King remarking that his predecessor
had 'in his proportion cheated beyond any accountant'). The
Castle was evidently much in need of repair, and Rewse was
authorised to spend £1,000 on it. Soon afterwards he added
another office, that of Receiver of Royal Aid for the Treasurer
of the Navy in the County of Oxford. But the authorities were
already discovering their mistake. Try as they would, they
could not get Mr. Rewse's accounts from him. When eventually he was arrested and brought to book, he was found to owe
the King £18,889. He seems soon to have been at liberty again

and died at Chalfont St. Peter in 1675. A certain obscurity which hangs over the history of Brudenells in this period arises largely from the many claims of creditors upon his estate. It was not until 1688 that James II decided (no doubt with a little prompting) that he might as well write off the debt still owing to the Crown, and that the man who had most claim to Dudley Rewse's estate in Chalfont was George, Lord Jeffreys.[47]

## JUDGE JEFFREYS

These villages have had many notable residents, but perhaps only one whose name everyone knows – Judge Jeffreys. A Welshman of the Welshmen, who claimed descent from Tudor Trevor, an eleventh-century Lord of Hereford, young George Jeffreys, when in 1663 he was admitted to the Inner Temple, found kinsmen there before him. An older cousin, Arthur Trevor, helped him and gave him the run of his chambers; and his first-cousin, John Trevor, had lately been called to the Bar. But George soon leaped ahead by his own charm, ability and pushfulness. At the age of 25 he was elected Common Serjeant of the City of London, and five years later was knighted and took silk.

Arthur Trevor had bought the Grange at Chalfont St. Peter in 1665, and two years later his nephew John inherited it. (This is the Sir John Trevor who became Master of the Rolls and Speaker in the House of Commons, and was said to have been as pure in the former capacity as he was corrupt in the latter.)[48] He adopted the Grange as his country house – his son Tudor Trevor was baptised in St. Peter's Church – and it was probably through visits to him that Jeffreys first became interested in this neighbourhood, and on the death of Ambrose Bennett of Hedgerley Bulstrode, bought that estate from Bennett's widow

44

and nephew. In the summer and autumn of 1676 he had a small army of labourers, glaziers, carpenters, masons and bricklayers at work, fitting up the mansion for his reception. There are builders' accounts for work 'don at Boulstrod House' and 'the letell house at Jarats Cras' (probably the original of 'Raylands Mead'). Amongst the materials used were £45-worth of bricks '2 iron cullums', '67 foot of Dutch tyles', 'Packthred', and '3,000 Lath nayles'. One contractor's bill came to over £70, to which he added: '14 weeks for myself-What you please'. Jeffrey's bailiff at Bulstrode at this time appears to have been Henry Tredway the Quaker, and one likes to imagine the two together.[49]

Jeffreys' wife died whilst the work was in progress. He had married for love a poor parson's daughter, and was devoted to her, and this must have been a sore loss to him. We know that he was at Bulstrode in August 1678, for in that month Charles II and some of his Court drove over from Windsor and dined there, and the King was so affable as to cause his host to 'sit down at the table with him' and 'drank to him seven times'.

## ELECTIONS

Jeffreys' promotion continued to be rapid and he soon became Lord Chief Justice, and a man to be feared. High Wycombe, for example, hastened to elect him Lord High Steward, thanked him profusely for his acceptance, and put up his coat of arms in the Guildhall. But he did not have things all his own way in Bucks. Macaulay tells the story of the election of a Member of Parliament for the County in 1685, when Jeffreys was determined to oust the Whig candidate, Thomas Wharton. The Tories tried to outwit the Whigs by switching the polling at the last moment from Aylesbury to Newport

Pagnell, and both parties poured out large sums in bribes: but 'the stout-hearted yeomen of Bucks.' rallied round, and Jeffreys' candidate was heavily defeated.[50]

## 'YOUR MONEY OR YOUR LIFE'

There are several tales of highwaymen associated with Bulstrode. The most circumstantial tells how a notorious highwayman called 'Old Mobb' stopped Lord Chief Justice Jeffreys not far from his house, disabled the two coachmen, and demanded money. 'Do you know who I am, sirrah?' asked Jeffreys. 'Yes, sir,' answered Old Mobb, 'I know you very well: and I ought by rights to charge you with a constable, for you once put me in great danger of my life – at Hertford Assizes. But I'm resolved to be even with you now'. At which, with a dreadful oath, he threatened to shoot, and the Lord Chief Justice handed over what money he had.[51]

## BULSTRODE REBUILT

It was not until later, after he had become Lord Chancellor at the age of forty, that Jeffreys rebuilt Bulstrode, which is said to have been badly damaged by fire in or about 1685. Tradition says that he lived at the Grange whilst it was being rebuilt, and this may well be true, for he had bought that house from his Trevor cousin five years earlier. He also bought, from Sir Roger Hill of Denham, the manor of Temple Bulstrode, thus uniting the two Bulstrode manors – Hedgerley Bulstrode and Temple Bulstrode.[52] The County Record Office has in its keeping a map of his estate prepared for him in 1686 by one John Fisher, which, besides being a beautiful example of the mapmaker's art, is of great topographical interest, showing the houses, the roads, and the field-names. For example, it shows Gerrards 'Cross' as the spot where the main road from Chalfont St. Peter to Windsor crossed the Oxford road, a road that now survives only as a footpath across Bulstrode Park, from Main Drive to the Hedgerley Lane gate, continuing by Mounthill lane to Stoke Poges and Windsor.

The engraving reproduced on page iv shows the gardens and the south front of Bulstrode substantially as it was rebuilt for Jeffreys. This imposing front, built of brick, extended 200 feet, with the principal rooms above, the bedrooms below. Behind it were two courts, separated by the hall of the old Tudor manor-house. Looking into the first court, and extending across its whole width, was what Horace Walpole called 'a brave gallery of old pictures'. From the end of this gallery opened the chapel, where in October 1687 Jeffreys' daughter Margaret was married, and in July of the following year his only surviving son John, a wild lad of 15, married Lady Charlotte Herbert, daughter of the Earl of Pembroke. The King and his counsellors wore wedding favours to celebrate the day, and a month later James II and his Queen, Mary of Modena, came to dine at Bulstrode.[53]

The end came quickly. In December the King fled the country, and Jeffreys was arrested, when trying to make his escape, and was imprisoned in the Tower, where he died in the following April. In his will, written in the Tower, he protests his undying loyalty to the Church of England, 'which I take to be the best Church in the world', and he expresses his anxiety for his children.[54]

## DUTCH HANS

Jeffreys might well have been anxious concerning his son 'Jacky' who got through a considerable fortune in a few years,

47

and was heavily in debt when he died in 1702. Four years later, his sister and her husband sold Bulstrode to a greater if less colourful personality – Hans William Bentinck, the Dutchman who had been the ever-faithful servant and friend of William, Prince of Orange, had nursed him through smallpox, suffered many wounds in his campaigns, become his most trusted diplomatic adviser, been the chief manager of the invasion in 1688, and had been created Earl of Portland and Viscount Woodstock when William and his wife Mary became King and Queen of England.[55]

Bentinck does not seem to have altered Bulstrode, save to complete the wings, shown in the view on page i, which Jeffreys had begun. He laid out the formal gardens, probably with the assistance of Henry Wise, who had served under him on the Royal Gardens, and added the Long Water, reminiscent of his Dutch Canals. To him we owe that straight stretch of the Windsor Road between the Packhorse and Hedgerley Lane. There is a document in the County Record Office, containing the signatures of a large number of local residents in 1707, consenting to his straightening the narrow and twisty road to Windsor 'by Widow Lane's farm'.[56] Nor let it be forgotten that he gave Gerrards Cross its first school, in Bull Lane, 'where are taught 20 boys and 15 girls, and all of them cloathed: two of the Children are put out Apprentice each year'. The Earl endowed it with £40 per annum – £20 for the schoolmaster, £20 for the schoolmistress.[57]

Bentinck, who was unhappily estranged from the King in his later years, and was never very popular with the English people, had resigned most of his public offices. But he was able to enjoy some years of comparative peace and domestic happiness at Bulstrode, at the close of his strenuous life. There his two youngest children were born; there in 1707 his daughter

48

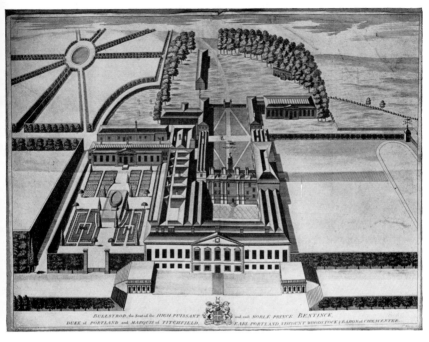

Bulstrode Park, late 18th century

The Grotto at Bulstrode, 18th century

Part of the plan of Bulstrode prepared for Judge Jeffreys in 1686

The men who built St. James' Church, Gerrards Cross, 1859

Bulstrode, South Front, about 1716

Chalfont Park, late 18th century

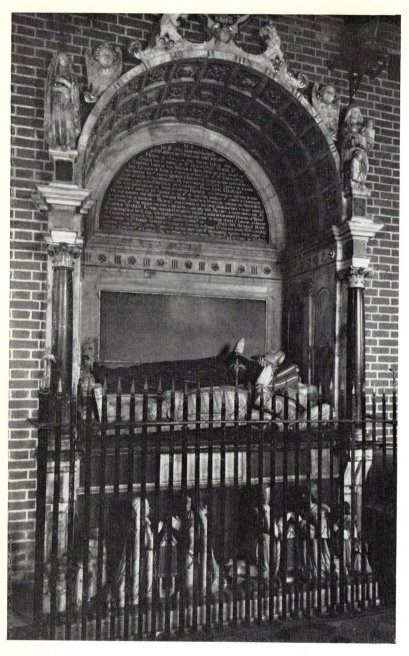

The Darrell tomb in Fulmer Church, early 17th century

The Misbourne River

Chalfont St. Peter, 1904

Frances married Lord Biron; there, in 1708, Queen Anne visited him; and there in 1709 he died.[58]

His son, the 2nd Earl, and afterwards 1st Duke of Portland – who also bought the Grange and its lands from Jeffreys' heirs – was responsible for a notable redecoration of the Chapel at Bulstrode, a complete scheme of Venetian wall-paintings, executed by Sebastian Ricci, one of the Italian painters who came to England to take part in the competition for the decoration of the dome of the newly completed St. Paul's Cathedral.[59]

## THE FALL OF THE CHURCH

We must return to the village of Chalfont St. Peter, upon which a sad calamity has fallen. One morning in July 1708, in a time of high winds and heavy rain, the tower of the Church crashed on to the nave and aisles (one suspects that those holes noted 70 years earlier had never been thoroughly repaired). The Vicar and churchwardens, surveying the ruins, evidently decided that the best course was to clear them away and start afresh. They were given leave to send out an appeal to all the parishes round about; but the money trickled in slowly: in January 1710, All Saints Hertford, sent £2 6s. 0d. and six months later, St. Paul's, Walden, contributed 1s. 3d. Browne Willis, the Bucks. antiquary, who visited Chalfont St. Peter at this time, found the church still in ruins, and the vicar, the Rev. Thomas Smart, bravely carrying on services in the chancel. What happened to the fabric of the old church – apart from those few stones now in the porch – does not appear; no doubt some was used in the foundations, and some in the tower, of the present church; other pieces have cropped up from time to time in private gardens.

Plans were prepared for a new church, rather smaller than

49

the old one (there were only 100 families in the parish) and at last building was begun. A summary of the final accounts survives:

| | | | | | | | |
|---|---|---|---|---|---|---|---|
| Joiners work | ... | ... | ... | ... | £100 | | |
| Blacksmith | ... | ... | ... | ... | 20 | | |
| Plummers | ... | ... | ... | ... | 100 | | |
| Glaziers | ... | ... | ... | ... | 10 | | |
| Brickers | ... | ... | ... | ... | 641 | 2 | 6 |
| Carpenters | ... | ... | ... | ... | 650 | 3 | – |
| Total | ... | ... | ... | ... | £1521 | 5 | 6 |

Eventually, in 1714, a handsome new Queen Anne Church was completed and consecrated. The mellowed tower and west end still proclaim its beauty, but the east end was altered, and not improved, in the 1850s.[60]


## OAKEND AND MARSHAM LODGE

Among the local gentry who contributed to the rebuilding, we may notice especially Henry Gould and John Wilkins.

Henry Gould was the fourth of that name to live at Oak End. His uncle (as mentioned above) was active for Parliament in the Civil War; and this Henry was born in the time of the Commonwealth, married Deborah, daughter of Thomas Whitchurch, Lord of the Manor of Chalfont St. Peter, and lived to become an eighteenth-century Squire, Justice of the Peace, and High Sheriff in 1704. He appears to have rebuilt Oak End about the turn of the century. Ever a staunch Whig and a faithful Churchman, he is described on his memorial in the church as 'amantissimus, utilissimus'.[61]

The parish register for 1700 records the baptism of 'Charles, son of John Wilkins, ironmonger, of Westminster'. John appears to have had a lease of the Grange from about 1700; but in 1714 he acquired the Chalfont Park estate. It was he who built Marsham Lodge, opposite Gerrards Cross Common, about 1727, apparently as a dower-house, on part of land called Walters Croft. (On another part of the same land a house was built, a few years later, where the Memorial Centre now stands.) He had also a house in Pall Mall, which, after his death in 1740, his widow let to Lord Berkeley of Stratton. She, we are told, had been a Miss Mary Drake, a distant relative of John Churchill, the great Duke of Marlborough, who had introduced her into the household of Queen Anne, with whom she had been a great favourite.[62]

## CHURCHILLS AT CHALFONT

Not long after her death, a nearer relative of Marlborough came to Chalfont. The Duke had a nephew, General Charles Churchill, who was much enamoured of a celebrated actress of the day, Ann Oldfield, by whom he had a son, another Charles Churchill. This Charles married in 1748 Lady Maria Walpole, Sir Robert Walpole's daughter by Maria Skerrett, the Irish charmer whom he subsequently married. The trustees of General Churchill's will bought for them, for £7,600, the manor of Brudenells, with the mansion-house called Chalfont House or the Old Place, a farm near it and the fields around, and also Oakgrove farm (near the site of St. Mary's School).[63] Lady Mary's half-brother, Horace Walpole the writer, visited them there, soon after they arrived, in company with his architect friend, John Chute. 'Last week,' he writes, 'we were at my sister's at Chaffont* in Bucks., to see what we could make of it: but it wants so much of everything, and would require so much more than an inventionary of £5,000, that we decided nothing, except that Mr. Chute has designed the prettiest house in the world for them'. A. L. Rowse, in 'The Early Churchills', writes: 'Horace did not take much to this match to begin with, but he shortly became great friends with this gay, untidy couple, and remained on excellent terms with them all their long lives. They never had any money, but this did not cramp their good humour or their enjoyment of life. When Horace grew old, they were the faithful ones who did not fail to come and spend an evening with him. Lady Mary Churchill (as she was called in spite of her birth) was at length provided for by being made housekeeper in charge of Kensington Palace, and subsequently of Windsor Castle'.[64]

What they and Mr. Chute did for the house can be seen from the picture on page v. It has suffered many alterations since, but we can still be grateful to them. Some of the work of Richard Bentley, another of Horace's architect-friends, can yet be seen. Walpole wrote in 1760: 'I have returned from Chaffont . . . Lady Mary is going to add to the number again. The house and grounds are still in the same dislocated condition: in short, they finish nothing but children: even Mr. Bentley's Gothic stable, which I call Houyhnhnm Castle, is not rough-cast yet.' A description put out shortly before the property was sold in 1794, runs: 'The House is old, and though low is pleasantly situated: and, as well as the Estate belonging to it, was considerably enlarged by Mr. Churchill, whose Taste also very much improved the Place, particularly in the judicious Disposition of the Water and the Grounds, and interspersing the latter with Plantations in a style of Elegant Simplicity.'[65]

* 'Chaffont' was the common pronunciation.

52

# THE DUCHESS OF PORTLAND'S BULSTRODE

Let Horace Walpole lead us back to Bulstrode, where he was a welcome, if critical visitor : 'I have been often at Bulstrode from Chaffont, but I don't like it. It is Dutch and trist. The pictures you mention in the gallery would be curious if they knew one from another; but the names are lost, and they are only sure that they have so many pounds of ancestors in the lump.' 'The chapel,' he wrote, 'was formerly decorated with the assumption, or presumption, of Chancellor Jeffreys, to whom it belonged; but a very judicious fire hurried him somewhere else.' The Duchess gave him nine portraits of the Court of Louis XIV : 'The Lord Portland brought them over, they hung in the nursery at Bulstrode, and the children amused themselves by shooting at them.'

The 2nd Duke of Portland, an amiable person known to his friends as 'Sweet William', had married a rich and intelligent wife, Lady Margaret Cavendish Harley, daughter of the Earl of Oxford : and in her time Bulstrode became one of England's Great Houses. We have glimpses of the place and its life in letters of her friends (and what letter writers they were !) and especially in letters of her bluestocking friends, Mrs. Elizabeth Montague and Mrs. Mary Delany.[66]

The Duchess had the collecting mania: trees, flowers and fungi, birds, beasts and fishes, books, paintings, and miniatures, busts, coins and medals, shells, rocks and fossils, 'English Insects and Exotic Insects' – she collected them all. (Not long before her death she 'collected' the famous Portland Vase now in the British Museum.) There is a pleasing description of a scurry round one day, to tidy away the books, papers and oddments that filled every chair, and then remove the comfortable chairs themselves, and 'set the blew damask chairs in prim form round the room', before the Princess Amelia arrived on a visit. Mrs.

Montague wrote: 'I believe the menagerie at Bulstrode is exceedingly worth seeing, for the Duchess of Portland is as eager on collecting animals as if she forsaw another Deluge, and was assembling every creature after its kind to preserve the species.' Mrs. Delany says: 'Mr Lightfoot and botany go on as usual: Her Grace's breakfast-room filled with sieves, pans, platters etc. on tables, windows and chairs.'[67]

The Rev. John Lightfoot, who combined the duties of curate at Uxbridge and domestic chaplain to the Duchess, deserves a special mention. He was one of the most distinguished naturalists of his time, a Founder-member of the Linnean Society, and a Fellow of the Royal Society. His detailed notes give the precise localities of many plants in Buckinghamshire and neighbouring counties, which are in many cases the first written records. He gives the first description of the Reed Warbler; the nest and eggs were brought by a fisherman on the Uxbridge river to Her Grace. He gives accounts also of several new species of freshwater snails. Of one of them it is said that it was found on the leaves of a certain iris in waters near Beaconsfield, by Mr. Agnew, gardener to 'the Duchess of Portland, by whose sagacity all the preceding shells were discovered, and by whose faithful pencil they were drawn.' As to flowers, we have the evidence of an observant traveller, Mrs. Lybbe Powys: 'The Duchess has every English plant in a separate garden by themselves' – a far remove from the formal gardens of earlier times.[68] As to the Park, Mrs. Delany is enthusiastic:

'Sunday after Chapel,' she wrote, 'the Duchess carried me a very pleasant airing she has had cut through a wood' [Dukes Wood] '3½ miles long, that joins to her park, and goes out on the Common, which from a brown, dreary-looking heath she will by her bounty and good taste make very pleasant.' And later the same day: 'A pretty, uncommon scene is now before

54

me on the lawn: a flock of sheep, shepherd and dog at a little distance, and in the foreground 15 or 16 hares, feeding with peacocks and guinea fowls.' And on a fine day in July, she writes that 'this place is like Paradise . . . Such woods, groves, lawns and terrasses, not to be described and all enlivened by such a variety of creatures, in perfect agreement – beautiful deer, oxen, cows, sheep of all countrys, bufaloes, mouflons, horses, asses, all in their proper places. Then hares and squirrels at every step you take, so confident in their security that they hardly run away.'[69]

One of her letters begins: 'The Order in which the King and Queen and Royal Family with their attendants went from Windsor to breakfast with the Dowager Duchess of Portland at Bulstrode on Wednesday, 12 August 1778, the Prince of Wales's birthday.' In mock Court Style, she lists the procession, and reckons that, with 33 servants, there were 56 personages in all – 'a splendid sight as they drove through the park and round the court, up to the house'. Breakfast was served in the Long Gallery: 'The Royals walked through the great apartment, admired everything they saw, the young ones full of observation, and proper questions, some skipping, some whistling and delighted above measure, and charmed with the excellent breakfast, and ate abundantly.' Afterwards the Queen admired Mrs. D's chenille work, and the King wanted to see her celebrated book of flowers, and fetched a chair for her. As she hesitated, 'Sit down, sit down', said the Queen, 'it is not everybody has a chair brought them by a King.' Mrs. D ventured to remark that it had long been her wish to see *all* the Royal Family. 'You have not seen them all yet', said the Queen, 'but if you will come to Windsor Castle with the Duchess of Portland, you shall see them altogether.' The very next evening Mrs. Delany was granted that happiness: first in the Queen's apartment at Windsor where the King and his seven sons came in to join the Queen and her five daughters; then, at a concert of music: and later, at a ball, 'begun by the Prince of Wales and the Bishop of Osnaburg dancing a minuet incomparably well'. (The latter was George III's second son, who had been appointed Bishop of Osnaburg in Hanover at the age of seven months.) It was midnight before Mrs. Delany got back to Bulstrode, after a blissful day, not nearly as tired as she had expected to be.[70]


## THE HUNT

She tells also of a morning in November when she and the Duchess rode in a chaise 'to Gararts Cross, about the middle of the Common', for a meeting of the Royal Staghounds. The King and Queen arrived soon afterwards, with their retinue ('among them Lady Mary Forbes, who took three rooms at the Bull Inn, and breakfasted 38 people'). The stag was brought in a cart, and let out on the Common.

Which reminds us of hunting as a local sport. It was not often that the Royal Staghounds met here (though as late as 1868 there was a memorable run via Denham, Pinner, and Wormwood Scrubs to Paddington Goods Station). But the foxhounds often met at Gerrards Cross. Indeed, there stood near the Packhorse until fairly recent times 'Huntsman's Hall', which was the kennels of the old Berkeley Hunt. An old account-book of the Hunt has an entry: '7 January – 20 March 1793. Thomas Oldaker's bills of wages, board and other expenses with the Whipers Inn, Helpers, Hounds and Horses at Gerrards Cross, £200 7s. $4\frac{1}{4}$.' Tom Oldaker, who built Berkeley Cottage on East Common, was a famous huntsman of the times, who died in 1831 at the age of 80, and remembered a run when hounds finally lost a fox in the rough ground in Kensington Gardens.[71]

## GOTT OF NEWLAND

One local hunting enthusiast was Sir H. T. Gott of Newland Park. Newland had belonged for a hundred years to the Saunders, a branch of a well-known Bucks. family: but they did not prosper there, and the property came eventually into the hands of money-lenders, from whom it was bought in 1770 by Henry Thomas Gott. Gott's name was originally Greening, and he appears to have been the son of George II's head gardener. Already a man of substance, he inherited a huge estate from two ladies of the Gott family of Battle (Sussex) and adopted their name. He evidently laid himself out to be the country gentleman, rebuilding the house, redesigning the gardens, serving for many years on the Committee of the Old Berkeley Hunt, as a Justice of the Peace, as Deputy Lieutenant of the County, and as Sheriff in 1774, when he was knighted. His wife had a Baronet-nephew who was for some time George III's Minister in Persia, and this Interesting Connection is remembered on a tablet in the Church. Many pleasant stories have been told about the curious obelisk which now stands by the entrance to Chalfont Colony: but no doubt the simple explanation is that Gott had it erected to show the way to his Mansion at Newland.[72]

## BULSTRODE'S PRIME MINISTER

Mrs. Delany reported, in 1776, a visit by 'the renowned Mr. Burke': the ladies decided that 'take him out of politics, he is very entertaining'. But in the time of the 3rd Duke of Portland, Edmund Burke, who lived at Beaconsfield, was often at Bulstrode, and no doubt more free to talk politics: for this Duke was much involved in the political fray for more than 40 years. Though not a brilliant man, he had a strong sense of public duty, and a gift for holding others together, and thus became in 1782–3 the head of the short lived Fox-North Coalition. But, like Burke, he hated the excesses of the French Revolution and feared its consequences here: and Bulstrode, which had been a great Whig House, became 'the headquarters of the Tory party'.* After Pitt's death, the Duke retired to Bulstrode; but he emerged again, reluctantly, in 1809 to become again Prime Minister for two harassed years before his death.[73]

In his time great changes took place at Bulstrode. Humphrey Repton, the celebrated landscape gardener, was from 1802–5 employed upon the gardens and park, and found here a job after his own heart, 'under the direction of His Grace, whose good taste will not suffer any part of that beautiful park to be disguised by the misjudging taste of former times'. He comments that upon the great work 'are occasionally employed among the more efficient labourers an hundred children from ten to fifteen years old, who are thus early trained to habits of wholesome industry . . . No object can be more delightful than the park scenery thus animated'. (One wonders about those children.)[74]

A year or two later, James Wyatt was commissioned to build a new house. Part of the south front was rebuilt, and a castellated Tudor-style wing took the place of the old west wing. But at this point the Duke's insecure finances caused work to slow down: £4,000 was owing to the architect, and soon building stopped altogether, not to be resumed until 1860.

* E. S. Roscoe, 'Penn's Country'.

All that now remains of Wyatt's house is the isolated 'Pigeon Tower', once the garden entrance to the house.[75]

## OVERSEERS OF THE POOR

Dukes, Knights, and Squires: but what of the common people? The eighteenth century was not so good for them: some farmers prospered, some small traders went under, many labouring men were often on poor relief. Times were especially hard for poor families on the road, seeking work, but the accounts of the Overseers of the Poor (which contain some remarkable spellings) show how well on the whole, the village, at this time, looked after its own poor. Two Overseers were appointed by the Vestry year by year, and the job was no sinecure. There were regular monthly payments to be paid to those on relief, always some families who needed fuel or clothing, poor children to be apprenticed (and sent out properly clad), sick folk to be nursed at home or taken to hospitals in London. Several entries refer to the village 'cage' (which stood behind the church); and there is a payment in 1726 'for a new pare of stocks & oyorn work & Cullering them'. In 1741–2 there was a smallpox epidemic, and those afflicted were isolated in an infirmary or 'pesthouse' which stood by Austenwood Common. When another (less virulent) epidemic occurred in 1759 some were accommodated in the house of the windmill, which was near the pesthouse.

An Act of 1697 required anyone coming into a parish to bring with him a Settlement Certificate from his former parish. This bore hardly on many poor people, and cost the parish a great deal in time and money. A curious case was that of two men who worked for John Hatch at Chalfont Lodge farm. The parish boundary ran through the house; but after looking

59

at a plan, the Justices decided that the men slept in Iver, and that Iver must be responsible for them.

## THE VILLAGE IN THE EIGHTEENTH CENTURY

Meanwhile the village was growing slowly: a few names and occupations may give a flavour of it:

Edward Ives, day labourer
John Russell, blacksmith
William Smith, currier
George Holder, waggoner
Henry Brown, cordwainer
William Nash, collar-maker
Thomas Hunt, maltster
Thomas Bradley, cooper
Henry Cooke, excise man
James Dakins, footsoldier
Thomas Price, miller
Andrew Burroughs, weaver
William Piner, brickmaker
John Bryant, sawyer
Edward Cawdery, carpenter[76]

Thomas Newman, glazier
Robert Hurles, thatcher
James Oakley, shoemaker
John Munke, barber and peruke maker
Robert Bennett, mercer
Henry Proud, higler
William Bonsey, tripeman
Richard Disborow, butcher
Thomas Dagger, tailor
Thomas Johnson, linen-draper
John Charsley, tobacconist
William Welling, sugarware potter

Besides these, of course, are the farmers, and an increasing number of victuallers. Thomas Piner, brickmaker, erected the Packhorse Inn and a smithy in 1708: and when the official Register began in 1753 there were (in addition to the inns already mentioned) the Kings Arms (kept by Henry Bennett), the George (Joseph Chitch), the Golden Ball (William Carter) and the Pheasant (then in Chalfont St. Peter). The Rose and Crown and the Waggon and Horses started life soon after this, and also the Fox and Hounds on the Oxford Road (now the Apple-Tree Restaurant). L. M. Wulcko in his pamphlet 'Some Early Friendly Societies in Bucks.' mentions a Chalfont Friendly Society which was started at the White Hart in Chalfont St. Peter in 1795, and another begun at the Greyhound in 1806.[77]

Tradition says that 'Woodhill', by the 19th milestone on the Oxford road, was also for some time a posting inn. This house and its lands formed part of property given by the Duchess of Somerset to Brasenose College in 1679 (from which benefaction Somerset Iver Scholarships are still awarded). The house was largely rebuilt in the eighteenth century and is said to contain a fine ceiling and staircase designed by the Adams brothers.[78]

The open-field system continued in Chalfont St. Peter until the nineteenth century (although Latchmoor Common Field was enclosed in 1847) and each year in the manor court it was decided which of the common fields should be sown, and which lie fallow. Throughout the eighteenth century successive Whitchurch Squires kept up their Manor Court in some style, appointing annually the constables, tithing-men, field-keepers and ale-tasters, and demanding headsilver from all their tenants. There are repeated injunctions to the landholders in Old Mead and Dewland Common to repair the ditches, banks, watercourses, stone bridges and ford: and several tenants are fined for removing soil from Gold Hill or bracken from Chalfont Heath. As the century goes on, incroachments upon 'Gerrards Cross Common' become more frequent, as new houses are erected: the original northern boundary of the Common may be judged from that piece of it which adjoins the old school.[79]

Church records show that the number of families in the village of Chalfont St. Peter grew from 100 in 1705 to 160 in

1723. They included only 2 or 3 Quaker, and 2 or 3 Presbyterian, households. Our Vicar at that time was also Vicar of Bisley in Surrey, but he and his curate maintained Services on Sundays, Festivals and 4–6 Holy Days, catechizing in Lent and Summer, and Holy Communion four times a year. The annual value of the living was increased by Queen Anne's bounty to £46 18s. 3¾d. 'The present Vicar,' adds Mr. Smart, 'takes 6d per house Easter offerings, not being able to get more, because the last vicar discontinued these for some years'.

The vicarage had been rebuilt in brick, and in 1707 was improved by the addition of 'a Necessary house, tiled and floored with deal, with two seats for men, and one for a child'.[80]

Owing to the church's connection with St. John's College, and that college's connection with Merchant Taylor's School, several of our vicars had been educated at that school and afterwards gained high academic honours. For example, Mr. Smart's successor, Moses Willes, was admitted to St. John's College from Merchant Taylor's in 1688, graduated in 1692, took his M.A. in 1696, and became Lecturer in Mathematics and a Fellow of the College in the following year. He then proceeded gently to B.D. in 1702, College Bursar in 1706, Vice-President in 1710, DD in 1711 and Dean of Divinity in 1712; and he remained a Fellow throughout his time at Chalfont St. Peter. However, it seems that these learned vicars and their curates carried out their necessary duties here; and one of them, at least, receives a glowing tribute on his memorial in the church – Dr. John Chalmers, 'a faithful pastor of this parish for 28 years'. In his time the vicarage was again rebuilt, and he was given leave to make an entrance to it from the main road, in place of that from Vicarage Lane. From his time, also, are dated five of the church bells, cast by Mears of Whitechapel.[81]

An Account of the Parish Church's belongings in 1783 is

62

simple, including two Surplices, one Bible folio, two Common Prayers folio, three Forms, and an Umbrella. The Bible and the more handsome of the big Prayer Books, inscribed with a fierce Lion Rampant, were given in 1717 by Arthur Trevor, son and heir of Sir John Trevor, Jeffreys' cousin mentioned above.[82] The Account adds:

> 'Mr. William Courtney, who died on December 5th, 1770, left an annuity of £400 stock in the four per cents, and the money arising from that annuity is to be dispos'd of in bread for ever for eleven poor unmarried women, eleven loaves one to each, and to the Clerk one, which are twelve to be given in the Church every Sunday after Divine Service. – Jho. Powell, Curate; Jn. Hunt, Jos Gurney, church wardens.'

Mr. William Courtney was a Rotherhithe maltster, who bought Tubbs farm; perhaps he was a son of the Robert Courtney who was churchwarden of St. Peter's when the Rebuilding Appeal was sent out in 1709. His Charity is still continued.

But a wind of change was blowing, that wind which found voice in Wesley and Whitfield. About 1772 Mr. George Woodward obtained a licence for meetings for worship at the Mill House, Chalfont St. Peter, and a few years later he built a chapel beside Gold Hill Common; its pulpit was supplied for a time by ministers and students of Lady Huntingdon's Connexion and its first minister was a Mr. Allen, who also kept a small school. A Meeting House on the present site was begun by Thomas Kean, and was opened in 1792, as an Independent Church. But in 1800 a Baptist became its minister; in 1807 it was recognised as a Baptist Church, and as such it still flourishes. There was also a Nonconformist congregation meeting at Horn Hill, in the house of William Gillibrand, Overs Farm.[83]

The turn of the century brought some notable changes amongst our gentry. In 1794 Chalfont Park was bought by Thomas Hibbert, in 1809 Thomas Allen bought Newlands, and in 1810 Bulstrode was sold to the Duke of Somerset. Mistress Ann, the last of the Whitchurches, died in 1809, and the Manor passed to her cousin, the Rev. William Jones of Chalfont St. Giles. The Hibberts, the Allens, the Somersets, and the Squire – these are our masters throughout most of the nineteenth century. In 1850 the Rev. William Jones was succeeded by his daughter Mary, wife of the Rev. Edward Moore; in 1885 Bulstrode passed to the Duke of Somerset's daughter, Lady Helen Guendolen, mother of Sir John F. Ramsden, Bart; in 1887 Chalfont Park was bought by Captain Penton.

Papers in the parish chest give some information concerning the village at this time. A Return demanded in 1831 shows that there were 180 inhabited houses, housing 686 males and 730 females. Of these, 149 were farm-labourers, 28 men-servants, and 61 female servants. There were also 2 manufacturers – perhaps the two potters, one in Potkiln lane, the other near Marsham lane. Petty sessions were held every three weeks at the Pheasant, and the Constables appointed by the Court Leet had to report there. There, in 1856, Daniel Russell, who had the mill just above the Greyhound, appealed against his assessment. The mill had been used at various periods to produce silk, flour, and felt; Daniel was using it to grind flour, and had installed steam-power.

The Overseers had paid Daniel Northcroft in 1825 for repairing the Church House and the Almshouses, and in 1836 for repairing the cage. But the Church House must have been demolished soon afterwards, for the site, the south-east corner of the churchyard, was levelled in 1849. 'The old dilapidated almshouses which adjoin the Church yard' were removed in 1864.

The Vicarage still had its farm buildings. In the Church, James Cole in 1819 was employed to repair the old gallery, and John Clark was paid a shilling a week for playing the bassoon. There are regular payments of 'Ringing beer' to the bell-ringers; but in 1856 it was decided that their beer money on May 29th and November 5th should not be paid out of church rates.

## 'A GOOD WORKHOUSE' AND BAD MANAGEMENT

Village affairs, in the first half of the century, were in the hands of a clique, who appear to have been more zealous for their own interests than for the public good. This less pleasant aspect of village life is well illustrated by the story of the Workhouse, a story which has some significance in the grim history of Poor Relief.

In 1825 the Churchwardens and the Overseers of the Poor of the Parish bought three cottages on the west side of the village street, and built on the site a Workhouse (which still stands, with its iron lamp-bracket). Ten years later (soon after Parliament had appointed Poor Law Commissioners) the experiment came to an ignominious end. The Inspector reported in no uncertain terms. The House, he said, was a good house, in very good repair: it could not easily be divided, but it would hold about 150 of one class, say, able-bodied men. At present, 'there are 35 in the house of all kinds, and amongst them two idiots'. 'This appears to be a very ill-conducted Parish: the Vestry is formed of small rate-payers and little shop-keepers. The Poor are farmed for £650 to the Master of the House,

65

and the Overseer, who is a little Butcher, supplies the Master with the Meat for the House. This Overseer had made a very incomplete return, and on my giving him a return paper to fill up, both he and the Master of the house said that they could not tell how many Poor there were, but it was a well-conducted Parish, and they could get on very well without the assistance of the Commissioners. The Master of the house and the Butcher-Overseer clearly understood one another very well and, at the expense of the Parish, did all they could to increase each other's gains. There was no attempt whatever to effect any classification – men, women, and children, sick and ill, and two lunatics, were all mixed together in the Chimney-corner. The Magistrates of this District, who are well acquainted with the state of this Parish, say that it is ill-conducted, that the jobbing is most infamous, and that of all the Parishes this most requires the interference of the Board'. In the following year, by Resolution of the Vestry, the Workhouse was sold.[84]

## THE HIBBERTS

The application for leave to dispose of the Workhouse was headed by J. N. Hibbert Esq. The Hibbert family has its memorials in St. Peter's Church, and its members deserve to be remembered in Chalfont St. Peter, to which they were notable benefactors. The family came from Marple (Cheshire) and had extensive interests in Jamaica.[85] John Nembhard Hibbert – of whom it is recorded that at the time of his death in 1885 he was one of the few survivors of those who had fought at the battle of Waterloo – gave land for allotment gardens, gave land for the extension of the churchyard, erected in the Amersham road 'buildings of plain Gothic architecture comprising an

Infants School and two Almshouses, each with rustic porch' (pulled down in 1962): and also gave and endowed our invaluable Cottage Hospital, opened by the Lord Bishop of Oxford in 1871. After Mr. Hibbert's death, the south porch of the Church was erected as a memorial to him.

The Hibbert Estate – 1037 acres – was broken up and sold in 1888. It included 'the Stately Mansion in Tudor style, with clock-tower and ivy clad turrets' (with the added attractions of 'capital wing – and ground-shooting, good trout – fishing in the Misbourne, and an Eel Weir at the lower end'): Chalfont Lodge (where some of the Hibberts lived); the Cottage Hospital; the Parish Room, formerly the Girls' School; Swan Farm and 155 acres, let to Mr. William Gurney of Chalfont St. Giles; Coldharbour and Oak End Farms; Isle of Wight Farm and 136 acres, let to Richard and Edward Davis for £115 p.a.; the Mill House and 40 acres; the Watercress beds; Lambscroft Farm in School Lane (occupied by Mr. Z. Lofty); and a meadow called Love's Delight (occupied by the Vicar).[86]


## NEW TENANTS AT BULSTRODE

Bulstrode we left in an unfinished state, when the Portland money ran out. The Duke of Somerset, when he bought it, soon called in architects to finish the rebuilding: Robert Smirke was there in 1811, and Jeffery Wyattville soon after. But nothing came of it; instead, large quantities of building materials were sold. But part of the house was habitable, and was let to various tenants. It was taken in 1841 by Colonel George Alexander Reid and his two sisters, who liked it well enough to renew their lease 7 years later, and to rent also Bulstrode Cottage in

Hedgerley lane (with the Little Park opposite), Pickerage House and farm at Fulmer, and Gerrards Cross farm (Manor Lane).[87]

The Reids were children of Andrew Reid Esq. of Lyonsdown, Barnet, and Liquorpond Street, London, a Scot who was for many years a principal partner in one of the largest porter breweries in London. George, after leaving Oxford, entered the 2nd Life Guards, which he subsequently commanded as Colonel. Soon after his election, in 1845, as Member of Parliament for Windsor, he resigned from active duties, but continued as an unattached officer. He was a director of the London and South Western Railway in its early days, but chiefly devoted himself to his parliamentary duties, and was greatly respected in Windsor, to which borough he was a notable benefactor.[88]

They were not easy tenants. Miss Louisa wrote most of the letters to the Duke's Agent; and she pours out a gentle stream of complaints and requests – for new buildings at Pickerage, bay windows at Bulstrode, a new conservatory, and so forth. The Colonel had evidently taken on more land than he could well manage. In the late 1840s, the Duke's bailiff reports most of the farms tenantless, and only a man and boy at work in the gardens. Mr. Allen of Moat farm, gave up the struggle: 'All my efforts to reconcile that poor meek-hearted young man to the present depressed times are quite unavailing.' Miss Louisa would have taken on that farm also: 'The distress of the labouring class around Bulstrode through the want of employment suggested to my sister the idea of taking the farm to afford the opportunity of being useful to the Poor on the Duke's Estate. To advance this object she is willing to encounter the many difficulties of the undertaking in the inauspicious aspect of the times; but there must be a consideration from you to enable us to carry it out.' However, the Agent did not think the prospects of the farming interest so gloomy that the Duke should forego the modest rent. 'And so', wrote Miss Louisa, 'we must abandon the pleasure, and Mr. Allen must seek a richer substitute . . . But in this locality there are no fewer than ten farms asking for tenants! So much for the prosperity of Bucks!'[89]

It should be added that the Duke had the reputation of being an exceptionally good landlord. Conditions soon began to improve, and the Reids turned to other projects – cut short, alas, by the Colonel's unexpected death in 1852.

## ST. JAMES

But now Gerrards Cross was beginning to emerge as a community, rather than merely a cross-roads. On August 30th, 1859, Samuel Wilberforce, Bishop of Oxford, consecrated the newly built Church of St. James. The Duke of Somerset gave the land, which had been part of Fulmer Common, and the Church was given by the Misses Anna Maria and Louisa Reid, of Pickeridge, Fulmer, in memory of their brother, Major General George Reid, M.P. (N.B. The first Vicar said in his first sermon: 'When the passing stranger inquires "Who taught that heaven-directed tower to rise?" your lisping babes shall articulate the names of your disinterested benefactors'.)

It was in 1856 that Miss Louisa, then living at Pickeridge, Fulmer, wrote to the Duke of Somerset's Agent, asking for a grant of Common Land for this purpose: 'We do not fear difficulties in carrying out our views as respects the Ecclesiastical arrangements, and Mr. Tite's good taste and judgement would secure His Grace's Manor from disfigurement.' The Agent, after consulting the Duke's lawyer, wrote:

69

'Maiden Bradley
7 May. 1856

'My Lord Duke,

I have been lately in correspondence with your Grace's
Lady Tenants, the Misses Reid, of Pickerage Bulstrode, who
have wished me to prefer their petition to your Grace that
you will grant them a site on Fulmer Common for erecting
a church at their *own entire expense*. Now at first it appeared
quite startling, as having some serious question whether your
Grace could make a valid conveyance of an *un*enclosed
portion of the Common, though within one of your Manors;
and therefore, not to trouble your Grace unnecessarily, I
applied to Mr. Jennings for his opinion, who considers your
Grace to have full power under the Church Buildings Act,
50 George III, and as the site – say, 2 acres – forms part of
the Common, not of any actual value, it would decidedly be
of advantage to your Property, as adding respectability in
that locality.

A site had been offered them, by the Lord of the next
Manor, but this seems more central, and meeting more
general approval. It seems the contemplated Building is to
be in commemoration of their Brother, the late General! I
should really respectfully say, there could be no possible
objection on your Grace's behalf, and it would be an ever-
lasting and distinct confirmation of your Title to the Manor.

The Ladies seem anxious for as early a reply as your Grace
could give.

I have the honour etc.
M. J. Festing'


The Duke replied promptly, readily acceding to the ladies'
request; negotiations were set on foot, Mr. Tite produced his
design (reminiscent, it is said, of Pisa, to which the General had

had a special attachment) and the building – carried out by Hardy & Sons of Cowley – was completed in 1858, although, owing to the Law's delays and the Bishop's engagements, it could not be consecrated before August 1859. It was a notable act of faith, for there were few houses near it; but the church served some in other parishes who lived at a distance from their own parish church, and in 1859 'the Consolidated Chapelry of the Church of St. James, Gerrards Cross', was created by Order in Council, embracing parts of Chalfont St. Peter, Iver, Fulmer, Langley Marish and Upton-cum-Chalvey. The eminent architect Sir William Tite, M.P., a friend of the Reids, certainly achieved something different from the usual run of Victorian Gothic. Experts of the time praised the originality and skill of his design: opinions concerning its appearance varied, then, as now.[90] The first vicar, the Rev. W. J. Bramley-Moore, son of John Bramley-Moore, Esq., M.P. of Langley Lodge, published a little book, 'The First Sabbath at Gerrards Cross', which contains the sermons preached on that first Sunday, a poem he had written about the church, an architectural description, and an 'Address to the founders of the New Church from the surrounding inhabitants', with a list of 300 of these inhabitants which includes many familiar local names. The first Vicarage, we learn, was 'Latchmoor'. A fuller account of the building of the Church and its subsequent growth is given in 'Gerrards Cross and its Parish Church' by E. Clive Rouse and J. Gordon Harrison, published in the Centenary year 1959.[90a]

## SCHOOLS

In J. J. Sheahan's 'History and Topography of Buckinghamshire', following a description of Gerrards Cross as a 'highly respectable place consisting of many genteel residences and

71

some cottages built on the verge of the extensive common . . . nearly 1,000 acres, mostly covered with heather and furze', we read: 'Opposite to the Church, a very neat building for a School, with residence for the teachers attached, is now (1861) in course of construction. The school building is in the form of a cross of equal length and breadth – measuring 32 feet each way exhibiting four gables.' The Rev. Edward Moore, of Stone Dean, Lord of the Manor of Chalfont St. Peter, gave the land for the school 'for the education of children and adults, or children only, of the labouring, manufacturing, and other poorer classes . . . in the Principles of the Established Church'; and the school gained a grant from the National Society, other substantial subscribers being the Vicar and the Duke of Somerset. The first teacher, who lived in the very small house adjoining the school, was Miss Jane James, who received £35 per annum, plus furnished house, fuel and light. After the 1870 Education Act, the number of scholars rose from 41 in 1870 to 93 in 1879. In that year Mr. Charles E. Colston was appointed headmaster. He came straight from college and continued as head until his resignation in 1920 – a long and notable career, both in the life of the school and in the life of the village, for he took an active part in public life.

In 'Gerrards Cross C.E. School 1862–1962', compiled by the present (1968) headmaster, Mr. Lewis J. Simpkin, are extracts, grave and gay, from the School Log Book, which help one to realize how different life was then, when there were no cars or bicycles, and Gerrards Cross was a predominantly agricultural area. For example:

'February 1865: Re-admitted L.S. and G.L. who had stayed away during the winter on account of the weather: both under 6 years old.'

'July 1863: Very poor attendance. The older children help in haymaking and fruit picking.'

The history of Chalfont St. Peter school is longer and more complex. As we saw, there had been a school in the Church House in the seventeenth century: perhaps it continued, intermittently, until the nineteenth, for in 1843 there was a 'National School' on that site. Ten years later, that had been pulled down, and a new school for boys and girls erected in 'School' Lane (schoolmaster, Joseph Marfleet), as well as the Hibberts' Infants' school which was noticed earlier. Besides these, the Rev. David Ives, the Baptist minister, kept a boarding school at Gold Hill House, Mary Northcroft (next door) had a day school, and there were other private schools, varying from Dames' schools at 2d. a week to superior establishments at 6d. per week.

As numbers increased, the girls of the National School transferred, first to the lecture room in Churchfield Road (given by Mr. Hibbert) and then to the Church Room (given by the Rev. G. M. Bullock). In 1892 Girls' and Infants' Schools were built on the present site, and in 1912 the boys moved from School Lane to an extension on the same site.[91]

## ROADS

The busy main street of Gerrards Cross, now full of cars, is named after the patient packhorse, and useful he must have been, throughout most of our history, when the roads were little more than cart-tracks. The eighteenth-century Turnpike Acts brought some improvement to the main roads, though as late as 1797 a traveller could report of the Oxford Road near Uxbridge that there was only one passable track on it, and that less than six feet wide, and eight inches deep in liquid mud. Not until the influence of the blessed Macadam spread in the 1830s was any substantial improvement made. Under the Turnpike Act of 1752, there was a toll-gate at Tatling End on the Oxford road: and, on the Wendover road toll-gates at Oak End and Gravel Hill. The Bull and the Greyhound were noted coaching-inns. It is said that at the Greyhound the coaches changed to broader wheels, seeing that tolls on the way to London were based upon the width of the wheels. For the rest, there was the useful carrier: in 1853, John Hunt left Chalfont St. Peter early every Thursday morning for the Angel in Farringdon Street, returning on the Saturday, whilst Thomas Shackell drove from Gerrards Cross to Clements Inn, Old Bailey. Until Gerrards Cross station opened in 1906, the nearest railway station was at Uxbridge, so that the carrier was much in demand. Gerrards Cross – what there was of it – then centred on the Bull, and the smithy and post office opposite, the little Post Office being a central office 'whence letter bags are despatched to surrounding towns and villages'. The office was a small attachment to 'Flint Cottage' (demolished in 1962) where for over 90 years the Matthews family also carried on a tailoring business. The present Gerrards Cross Post Office was built in 1912.

Roads sometimes fade away; the main road from Chalfont St. Peter to Beaconsfield used to lie along Layters Lane, and thence by what is now only a cart-track called Mouse Lane to 'Wilton's Green', now enclosed in Wilton Park. An eighteenth-century owner of Wilton Park extended the park, diverting the Oxford Road, closing some lanes that ran through the park, and making that straight road from A40 to Jordans which is known as Potkiln Lane, from the old-established pottery there.[92]

74

Since the break-up of the old estates and the coming of the railway many new roads have been constructed; and the names of some of them happily perpetuate the old field names, such as Hither Meadow, Garners End, Foxdell Way, Winkers Close and Howards Wood.

## ORCHEHILL

One estate sold early in the present century was that of Orchehill.[93] Orchehill House (now St. Mary's School) was the home of William Blount, who married Lady Charlotte, sister of the 12th Duke of Somerset. Their park extended from Marsham Lane to Claydons Lane, and one lodge may still be seen at the junction of South Park Drive and the Amersham Road. Another is still to be seen at the far end of Bulstrode Way, whence a drive, known as Lady Charlotte's Drive led across the fields and the Packhorse Road to Orchehill House. William Blount and Lady Charlotte are commemorated in the east window of St. James's Church.

## THE GENERAL

A notable figure in Chalfont St. Peter in the first half of the nineteenth century was Lieutenant General Terence O'Loghlin, a veteran of the Napoleonic wars, who had been wounded at Tournai in 1793, and subsequently commanded the Brigade of Guards under Wellington in the Peninsular War. He bought the Grange in 1802 and lived there until his death in 1843. He has his memorial tablet in the Church, and also his vault, which he is said to have sampled not long before his death.[94]

75

## MAYNE REID

Amongst the congregation at St. James in its early years might have been noticed a swarthy gentleman, with black imperial and mustachios, a dandy in his dress, with lemon kid gloves, who generally appeared to be more interested in the ladies' bonnetts than in the Service. This was Mayne Reid,[95] adventurer, soldier, and writer of a large number of romances and boys' stories, once immensely popular. (Connoisseurs should sample 'The White Gauntlet', a romance which has its setting in this locality in ye olden times.) He had lived and fought in Mexico, and he built in 1866 beside the Oxford Road (near Huesden Way) a 'rancho' in the Mexican style. Unfortunately, further building speculations at Gerrards Cross involved him in heavy loss and in 1867 he returned to the United States.

## THE COLONY

A notable newcomer was the National Society for Epileptics which in 1894 purchased Skippings Farm, with £4,000 given by J. Passmore Edwards, Esq. Tubbs Farm and Roberts Farm were added later, and the Colony today consists of an estate of over 350 acres, including its own farm, orchard and market gardens, a self-contained community where 500 men and women are accommodated in 19 separate houses, and are trained, employed, and cared for.

## THE TWENTIETH CENTURY

An elderly resident of Gerrards Cross who as a boy attended the school on the Common, recalls a day when the headmaster

76

said: 'I have heard that a Motor Car is to come along the Oxford Road this afternoon: if you behave yourselves, you may go across the Common, and watch it go by.' It was behind schedule, but before they saw it they could hear it chugging along the quiet road.

The motor car and the railway have brought great changes. George Stephenson had a scheme for a railway from London to Aylesbury, but it did not materialise, and it was not until 1904–6 that the Great Central and the Great Western jointly constructed the line through High Wycombe. In the Gerrards Cross section this involved building a high viaduct and digging a long and deep cutting, and the imported navvies who worked on the job are still remembered. They had their hut dwellings, their Navvies Mission, and their 300 pints waiting for them at the Packhorse when they knocked off. The contractors were Messrs. Paulings, and the station was opened in 1906.

The deep cutting complicated the main drainage scheme carried out in 1910–11. The surveyor stated then that the number of houses in Gerrards Cross had increased from 75 to 325 in four years, and he based his scheme on 500 more. The extensive development in recent years south of the Oxford Road does not seem to have been then contemplated.

Another change was a strange work of nature. In 1911 Gerrards Cross Common was on fire and burned for three months. Before that time it had been a wide open stretch of heather and gorse: afterwards the silver birches sprang up everywhere, and the Common became a pleasant woodland, in which it is hard now to find a sprig of heather.[96]

## THE NEW PARISH

The first Annual Meeting of Gerrards Cross Parish Council[97] was held on November 25th, 1895, when Colonel the Hon.

W. Le Poer Trench, C.V.O., R.E., of St. Hubert's, was elected Chairman. The Ordnance Survey Department was asked to send two representatives to perambulate the bounds of the new parish. Mr. Witham was appointed meersman on behalf of the parish, and the boundary posts were eventually put up ten years later. It was proposed to celebrate the Coronation of King Edward VII by planting an avenue of trees across the Common from the cross-roads to the Packhorse, subject to the consent of the Lord of the Manor and the copyholders (who had common rights): but the Lord of the Manor was far from enthusiastic, and no one could or would tell who the copyholders were. The emptying of cesspools was a co: tinual headache, as the community grew, and in 1910 a Steam Motor Exhauster was purchased. But it was generally believed that sparks from this unlucky machine started that fire on the Common, and it was sold again two years later. Chalfont St. Peter was asked to join in the main drainage scheme, but did not think that necessary. The arrival of the railway contractors caused some anxieties; additional Parish Constables were appointed, and the General Post Office was asked to supply a bicycle, to expedite the delivery of telegrams.

Even before the station was opened, development began: Marsham Way and Woodlands, Bulstrode Way and Orchehill Avenue were constructed. Chalfont St. Peter proposed a Joint Voluntary Fire Brigade, but Gerrards Cross did not think the time opportune. A serious fire occurred in Oak End Waye in 1913, and another in Station Road in the following year. It was discovered that there were not enough hydrants, those there were could not be found; when they were found they were buried under some inches of road; when they were dug out the key was not available; when the key was found there was insufficient pressure of water. However, Uxbridge Fire Brigade was summoned, and arrived in less than an hour. In

1908 a proposal to obtain control of the Common was put forward. The Parish Council worked at this for years, before in 1920, control was at last gained, and suitable bye-laws accepted. In that year, Chalfont St. Peter suggested that the two parishes might become one Urban District Council area, but Gerrards Cross did not think the time opportune. In 1912 a scheme for the administration of the Chalfonts and Gerrards Cross Cottage Hospital was amended by the Parish Council, in order to maintain the right of local doctors to attend their own patients in the hospital.

## THE BRIGHTON OF BUCKINGHAMSHIRE

It is interesting to turn the pages of directories and guide-books of a few years ago. Gerrards Cross is called 'the Brighton of Bucks.', with reference to its health-giving quality, 300 feet up, with a deep gravel soil. 'The water from the village pump on Gerrards Cross Common was noted for its curative powers for those suffering from rheumatism, and people from distant places used to make a pilgrimage to drink it.'

In 1907, when the Latchmoor Estate was being developed, we are told: 'As for communication with London, the fact that Mr. Sam Fay, J.P., the general manager of the Great Central Railway is a resident of Gerrards Cross should be sufficient security on that score. The Station is only 27 minutes from Paddington or Marylebone, and it is even said that the latter terminus will be attainable in 17 minutes when the new line is in complete working order.' A quarterly season ticket then cost £3 1s. 0d. 'but this will be considerably reduced, and the service improved, as the district develops'. 'The modern bugbear of rates and taxes can have no terrors in this parish, for the local rates are as low as anywhere in the kingdom, being only 4s. 4d. in the £'. 'The style of architecture of the residences is for the most part of that quaint domestic type so characteristic of Buckinghamshire . . . For £650 upwards a splendid residence can be secured, standing in its own grounds.' Twenty years later, when land at £100 per acre is still obtainable, it is stated: 'It is one of the features of the district that all the good class property is grouped in one part and the artisan type in another part.'

Chalfont St. Peter also was developing rapidly. Soon after the coming of the railway, the Common Downs estate was opened up, on the former common field of that name; the Petersville estate, north of the village, followed in 1921; and not long afterwards the Swan farm lands were sold for building, and became the Chalfont Heights estate. New building continues, especially in the Chalfont Common area. Now (in 1968) the by-pass road, planned many years ago, has recently been completed, and a new shopping centre in the village is being built. These developments, together with the creation of a car-park on the site of the old vicarage, have gone far to change the nature of the place. According to the 1968 figures, the population of Chalfont St. Peter was 13,980 and of Gerrards Cross 6,257.

## DEVELOPING COMMUNITIES

As the villages grew, a host of social activities began to develop. The golf course in Chalfont Park was laid out in 1921; the Hockey Club (President, Sir John Ramsden, Bart, of Bulstrode) also played in the Park, where the big House was now a residential hotel. Gerrards Cross Cricket Club (President, Colonel Le Poer Trench) played on the Common, opposite the Bull; the Chalfont St. Peter Cricket Club, in Newland Park. Their President was H. A. Harben, Esq. of Newland, who was Chairman of the Prudential, one of the pioneers of industrial assurance, and a generous benefactor to the Village, who gave the Hall at Horn Hill. The miniature Rifle Club had its outdoor range on land belonging to Sir Sam Fay of Raylands Mead. The Gerrards Cross and Chalfont St. Peter Fire Brigade had been formed in 1914, as the result of a public meeting called by Mr. C. P. Lovell, after that serious fire in Station Road. 'Since the sale and conversion of the Town Hall into a Garage,* the amusements of Gerrards Cross have become entirely centred in the Oak End Hall and Assembly Rooms centred in Oak End Waye.' Gerrards Cross at this time had no 'Picture Palace', but there was one at Chalfont St. Peter.

In Chalfont St. Peter, St. Pauls Chapel-of-Ease at Horn Hill had been built in 1866. In 1914, All Saints Church in Oval Way was consecrated, and in the following year, St. Joseph's Catholic Church by Austenwood Common (rebuilt and enlarged in 1962). A Methodist Church was opened in Oak End Way in 1912 (and a new church built on the same site in 1960) and the Congregational Church in Packhorse Road was opened in 1922, the Hall being added eight years later.

The names of those who gave their lives in two World Wars are commemorated on War Memorials in the two villages. After the first war, a Memorial scheme was put forward in Gerrards Cross for the purchase of the Vicarage (formerly 'Watercroft') and grounds of nearly three acres, for a Social Centre: but it was not until after the 1939–45 War that this was accomplished. The house (since extended) is now the home of an active Community Association, and in the entrance-hall a plaque bears these words:

'In loyalty to the memory of those who gave their lives in the war of 1939–45, this Centre is dedicated to the fostering and

* In Station Road.

furtherance in good fellowship of all arts and exercises healthful and enriching to body and mind, to the end that by the grace of Almighty God we, the living may together cultivate in the spirit of true community, the national heritage preserved for us and for our children at so great and sacred a cost.'

In Chalfont St. Peter, a Memorial Hall was built at the lower end of Gold Hill Lane. This was demolished, when the dream that some had long kept in mind was realised by the building, in 1962, of a fine new Community Centre, with hall, canteen, and smaller rooms, on the playing fields north of the village; and this is now in full use.

With so large an increase in population, the Chalfont St. Peter Primary School, under its headmaster, Mr. S. H. Bagley,[98] needed to increase its accommodation, and a new school also was opened in 1963 in the Chalfont Common area. A Secondary Modern School, 'Old Jobs', was opened in 1947 and under the direction of Mr. G. F. Horley has advanced both in quantity and quality; in 1961 the first part of its new buildings in Narcot Lane was opened, designed by the County Architect, Mr. F. B. Pooley. Numerous private schools also flourish, and Gerrards Cross' long-promised new Primary School has (in 1968) recently been completed.

Newcomers, who are unaware when they pass out of Chalfont St. Peter into Gerrards Cross, are sometimes puzzled by the parochialism of the two villages, which is accentuated by the fact that Chalfont St. Peter belongs to one Rural District (Amersham) and Gerrards Cross to another (Eton). Proposals to amalgamate the two villages have been talked of for years.

'Newland' is now a teachers' training college, 'Chalfont Park', research laboratories, and 'Bulstrode' the home of the World Evangelisation Crusade. In the villages, modern shops and multiple stores have arrived, and some light industries have their works. With the tentacles of London reaching out ever further, and the volume of motor traffic ever increasing, local councils have struggled valiantly at times both to provide more housing and also to preserve something of the village character of Chalfont St. Peter and Gerrards Cross, surrounded, as they are, by 'Green Belt' land; and this struggle continues.

'True community needs roots in the place in which we live, and in our common history and heritage.' Towards the growth of such roots, these pages are offered.

## WHAT NEXT?

'True community needs roots in the place in which we live, and in our common history and heritage.' It also requires participation in the present, and purpose for the future. To these ends (forsaking the rôle of historian) I venture to add these reflections :

1. One of the most obvious changes is that of land use. Even seventy years ago, this was almost entirely an agricultural and pastoral area. Now, the landed gentry have virtually been eliminated; and although several farms still operate on the Green Belt land which surrounds these villages, and there is land set apart for sports which is fully utilised, and the area is rich in gardens (in which many work wonders), still more and more land is covered with buildings. Many of these are costly homes; but there is a continuing demand for Council houses, and for owner-occupied houses at a moderate price. With building land at more than £10,000 per acre, there has been much in-filling, a greater density of building, and some taller blocks of flats and offices are beginning to appear. There has been some unnecessary destruction of good old buildings, and not all the new building is good to look at. There is need for local thought and care, if these villages are not to lose their character, and become just like every other suburb. Whether pressure of population will lead to re-classification of some of the Green Belt area remains to be seen.

83

The creation of a New Town in North Bucks. may, for a time, relieve the pressure on this area. But the issue will depend partly on wider plans to restrict London's spread, and partly upon the will of local residents to stop their amenities being nibbled away, and their villages swallowed up.

The interesting plan now under consideration to make a regional park of forty square miles along the Colne Valley, mainly for sports, would plainly have some effects upon these villages. (It might even modify the practice, followed by scores of families, of leaving this beautiful neighbourhood every summer weekend, to seek their pleasures elsewhere.)

No doubt there will be some small increase of industrial use. Already these villages have some crafts which have a wide reputation. Some have told their story elsewhere in this book; and there are others, such as JWB Engineering (which makes filters of various types) and the Bee Research Association at Hill House, through which the name of Chalfont St. Peter is known in many lands.

2. There were advantages and disadvantages in the old English village where bigger houses and smaller houses were mixed together, everybody knew everybody, and everyone worked in or around the village. But at least a sense of the community was a part of each person, for it had grown through the centuries. The situation is different today, when few work in the place where they sleep, many scarcely know their neighbours, and working-class housing is segregated from the rest. These handicaps can only be overcome by an active neighbourliness. Of this, there is much in these villages, though there is always room for more. A remarkable number of societies have grown up, in which residents can meet together for some common purpose and for social intercourse. The Memorial Centre at Gerrards Cross and the Community Centre at Chalfont St. Peter hum with activities, and are

extending their premises. Some of their affiliated organisations serve some particular local good cause, such as the Hospital, the Cheshire Home, or the Ponds Home for Spastics; a few (but not enough) have a wider outlook—such as Shelter, and the U.N.A. branch. Between them, they raise an astonishing amount of money for charities, and give a good deal of personal service. Some of these bodies, such as the Rotary Club and Round Table, serve both villages; as also does the Old People's Welfare Committee, which is keenly aware of the need for more accommodation for old people here.

3. Throughout past generations, the Church has been the chief 'community centre' (as well as bearing witness to Him from whom all true community derives). In a changed society, the Church is still for many a place of friendship in common purpose, and by its wider outlook helps to correct any tendency to self-complacency. But the variety of 'churches' now tends to create a number of groups separate from one another, according to village, and according to denomination. It is to be hoped that the formation of a Chalfont and District Council of Churches will help to overcome this fragmentation. Its area extends from Seer Green to Denham, and from Chalfont St. Giles to Fulmer, and its membership includes nearly all the local Catholic and Protestant Churches.

4. Schools, of course, play a great part in the life of a community. Here there has been a great development since the years when seventy boys and girls, segregated by a curtain, met in the National School at 'Penny Oak' in School Lane. Today the pupils in the four Junior Schools number about 950, the Infants Schools about 350, and the Chalfonts Secondary School about 550. The provision still falls short of the rise in population; in particular, there is need of a secondary grammar school in this area. In addition, there

are private schools for boys and for girls, which have a wide reputation, some nursery schools, and crêches at the two Centres. Youth Clubs and Youth Organisations provide for many of our young people; but there is room for further work in this field. Both villages have thriving Evening Institutes, where a large variety of subjects may be studied and enjoyed. Painting flourishes, but music and drama have a harder struggle.

5. It would be ungracious to end any review of the years without appreciation of the improvements which have come to this neighbourhood through the work of the Local Authorities, their councillors, officers, and employees, and of the local magistrates and police. What the administrative unit of the future will be can only be matter of speculation, at a time when all local government areas are under review. Gerrards Cross and Chalfont St. Peter make up one centre of population; but, at present, in most fields, there is a lack of co-ordination between them which is frequently absurd. That there should be healthy rivalry between the two villages is always to be desired; but that the one should not know what the other is doing, profits no one. It may be that the two will combine to form one unit; or a more viable unit might be formed of the two Chalfonts (excluding Little Chalfont). Gerrards Cross, and Fulmer, the present population of which is about 27,000. If the proposed new Parliamentary divisions are set up, this would be another boundary between Gerrards Cross and Chalfont St. Peter. Politically, South Bucks. has long been reckoned a safe Conservative seat; this fact does not make for intense political activity. Meanwhile (as our elected Councillors would agree) there is always need for vigilance, and for service, at the level of Parish, Rural District, and County Councils.

October, 1968.

# NOTES

I have not thought it necessary to repeat references given in Victoria County History of Bucks. (V.C.H.).

B   Bulstrode mss. (B.R.O.) (Ref. D/RA).
BAS   Bucks. Archaeological Society, County Museum, Aylesbury.
BRO   Bucks. Record Office, County Offices, Aylesbury.
(C)SPD   (Calendar of) State Papers, Domestic (PRO).
CSTP   Chalfont St. Peter.
DNB   'Dictionary of National Biography'.
GX   Gerrards Cross.
MR   Records of Manor of CSTP (BAS).
PCC   Will at Somerset House.
PRO   Public Record Office.
Records   'Records of Buckinghamshire'.

1. R. H. Lathbury : 'History of Denham'. W. H. Ward and K. S. Block : 'History of Iver'. R. E. Lloyd : 'Church and Village of Fulmer'.
   H. Adams Clarke: 'Parish Church of Chalfont St. Giles'.
2. The 1876 6-in. O.S. map is useful. Tithe map of 1843 at Tithe Redemption Office, Worthing.
3. 1924 excavation of the Camp: Records xi, 283. Names: Mawer and Stenton, 'Place-Names of Bucks.'. Kilns:

Records xiii, 252 and xiv, 153. Roman Roads: Viatores, 'Roman Roads in S.E. Midlands' (1964).

4. Domesday entries: VCH i, 235, 270. Manorial history: VCH iii, 195, 280, 297. The Turvilles: G. H. Fowler, 'Pipe-rolls of Bucks. and Beds.'.

5. Records xvii, 20ff.

6. VCH i, 391: Bucks. Feet of Fines (Bucks. Record Society, Vol. IV): Berks., Bucks. and Oxon Archaeological Society, xi.

7. Feet of Fines, 9 EdII, 18 EdII: Records xiv, 23: Inquisitions post mortem, 1300, 1342 and (Henry Drury) 1617 (PRO).

8. Mrs. Elvey's invaluable article is based mainly upon an excellent collection of manorial records, belonging to the Rev. P. C. Moore, and deposited on loan with BAS. See also Missenden Cartulary (ed. J. G. Jenkins) especially ii, 174ff.

9. Before 1330 the king had granted these lands to the Abbess of Burnham, who complained that Geoffrey and others broke her house, the spindle and iron of her mill, and her hedges there, cut her corn, consumed her grass, carried away timber, assaulted her steward, and so threatened her that for a long time she could get no one to serve her. (Close Rolls, 1330). Geoffrey was still fighting the case in 1346.

10. There is a useful sketch-map of the common fields in J. E. G. Bennell, 'Notes towards a history of CSTP' (Typescript in local libraries).

11. PCC, Luffenham 31. On Chantry: VCH iii, 197. 'The chantry standeth in the churchyard' (Records xiii, 200) Mr. Bennell tells me there are references in 1727–8 to a house in CSTP 'formerly called the Chantry house'.

12. I. S. Leadem: 'Domesday of Inclosures', 190, 206.

12a. Records xviii, 73, 96

13. VCH Herts, ii, 383. Patent Roll, 7Ed VI, pt. 13.

14. See index refs. in VCH and CSPD.

15. BAS has a manuscript 'Book of Bulstrode' by H. W. Bulstrode. There was a branch of the family at Beaconsfield; and it appears from PCC wills of Sir William (1527) and Maude (1531) that Sir William had a lease of Temple Bulstrode.

16. G. Redford and T. H. Riches, 'History of Uxbridge' (1818) pp. 205ff. PCC Mellershe 55.

17. 'Notes and Queries', 1863, pp. 150, 162.

18. A. Campling: 'The Family of Drury'.

19. Records xvii, 189.

20. CSPD, 1601.

21. VCH iii, 280. BAS have several court-rolls and lists of tenants of Temple Bulstrode manor, which included lands at Tring, Ford, Stone, Wexham and Clewer.

22. MR35.

23. Samuel Aldridge's will, in 1652, refers to 'my house & lands in a common called Austen wood in CSTP, which I bought of Thomas Bulstrode esq.' (PCC, Bowyer 154) On Mumfords and Ashwells, 'Historic Monuments Commission', i, 85.

24. Records, xv, 87.

25. CSPD 1577, cxv.

26. On the Manor of the Vicarage, see a characteristically careful article by Mr. John Bennell, Records, xvii, 392.

27. Bucks. Sessions Records (1678–94), 422, 434: B 1/60: Records, xvii, 186.

28. Records, xvii, 416; xviii, 97.

29. F. C. Eeles: 'Edwardian Inventories', Bucks., p. 44.

30. MR, 28: Records, x, 408: PCC, Pynning, 41.

31. DNB: J. Foster, 'Alumni Oxoniensis'.

32. Glebe terrier (Lincoln) and Tithe map. Some terriers are in BRO, some in Lincoln R.O.

33. CSPD: R. E. Lloyd, Fulmer: 1/223: Records, xv, 37 and xvii, 208.

34. SPD, 16/336. Some records of this enquiry are printed in Records vi, 154, 245.

35. SPD, 287/31. Some of these interesting letters are printed in Records, vii, 97.

36. B 2/13. Pennington's purchase included Chalfont Lodge farm and the Swan inn.

37. On Pennington, see DNB: Mary Keeler, 'The Long Parliament': and especially Valerie Pearl, 'London and the Outbreak of the Puritan Revolution'.

38. 'Walker Revised', ed. A. G. Matthews.

39. The House of Commons in September 1643 appointed John Chidwick; but Henry Gould's will, written in October 1644, and witnessed by both Chidwick and Holl, refers to 'my loving friend Thomas Holl, our minister in CSTP' (W. A. Shaw, 'English Churches under the Commonwealth', ii, 295: will in BRO). Thomas Holl B.A. was ordained priest by the Bishop of Oxford in 1614, and had been for some years vicar of Cholesbury, co. Bucks. (Lincoln, L.C. 5, p. 132 and Registers).

40. CSPD and Civil War Tracts.

41. 'Survey of Livings', 1650 (PRO, c. 94): W. A. Shaw, op. cit.: Mr. E. J. Briden kindly transcribed and sent the entry from Chesham Parish Church register.

42. On the early Quakers here, see Ellwood's Autobiography: Bucks. Record Society, volumes I and VII: W. H. Summers, 'Jordans and the Chalfonts'. On Milton's acquaintance with the Bulstrodes, Penningtons and Ellwood, see Masson's 'Life of Milton'.

43. T. Butterfield, PCC 1655/291: Wetherly (1641), Monk

(1649), Cawdrey (1639), Good (1647), all at BRO.

44. On Mumfords, note 23 above. The Whitchurch wills illustrate the progress of the family, and of the house: Richard, 1647 (BRO): Thomas, 1691 (PCC, Fane 159): Richard, 1709 (PCC, Young 224). On the Church House affair, Chancery Petty Bag, Charity Inquisitions 28/23 (PRO).

45. Glebe terrier, 1724 (Lincoln).

46. St. John's College Muniments, xli, 1 to 17.

47. CSPD 1666–76 : Treasury Book 1669 et seq. Fulmer deeds, BRO : CSTP register.

48. B 2/20, 2/25. On Trevor, DNB and Le Neve's 'Knights' : register, baptism.

49. Articles by H. M. Balfour in 'Law Journal', 1929. G. W. Keeton in 'Lord Chancellor Jeffreys and the Stuart Cause' points out that it is difficult to penetrate to facts about Jeffreys, and that Macaulay's well-known pen-portrait is based upon heavily-biased Whig sources.

50. 2nd Ledger Book of Chipping Wycombe, 1685. Macaulay's 'History of England', c. iv.

51. Alex. Smith: 'Lives of the . . . Highwaymen' (ed. 1926), p. 41. See also pp. 140ff.

52. B 1/44.

53. H. M. Hyde, 'Judge Jeffreys'. There are elevations and a plan on Fisher's map.

54. PCC 1690/130. But see note 49 above, and Luttrell's Diary.

55. B 1/60. On Bentinck, M. S. Grew, 'William Bentinck and William III'.

56. B 1/66. Jeffreys in 1686 had been given leave to divert Hedgerley lane (CSPD, May 12).

57. Camden's 'Britannia' (1720); Speculum CSTP (Lincoln RO). When Portland sold to Somerset in 1811, the deed

refers to Schoolhouse field and John Appleton, school-master. Schoolhouse field, in Bull Lane, was part of 'Ray-lands Mead' estate. (Information from the late Mr. E. G. Eardley Wilmot, and B 1/108.)

58. Hedgerley parish register. Historic Manuscripts Commission, Portland, iv, 504.
59. On the architectural history of Bulstrode, see a valuable article by John Harris in 'Architectural Review', November 1968, also W. H. Wadham Powell in 'Home Counties Magazine', vol. IX (1907–8).
60. Records, xi, 60. The church was well restored in 1966.
61. Ward and Block's 'Iver'.
62. CSTP ratebook (Parish chest): Burke's Commoners, s.v. W. Palmer: BRO deeds, CSTP and Fulmer: PCC, Browne 237, Lisle 30: Treasury Book 1715: Foster, Oxford Alumni. Mr. Wilkins was dilatory in paying his local rates: 'Spent at ye Packhorse when Mr. Wilkins was strained, 3s.' (Overseers' Accounts, 1740).
63. Neither is to be confused with Charles Churchill (1734–64), son of an Essex clergyman, poet and member of the Hellfire Club. Mr. L. M. Wulcko kindly communicated the substance of three Private Acts relating to this settlement: 23 Geo. II, c. 18; 19 Geo. III, c. 53; 32 Geo. III, c. 39. The property bought from Lister Selman Esq. in 1755 included, besides Chalfont Place or the Old House, another house on the S.E. side of it, a farmhouse, and a limekiln: but the other house, farmhouse and limekiln had been demolished before the property was sold in 1794. Oakgrove farm and 71 acres Lister Selman had bought from Robert Hill, blacksmith.
64. 'Walpole's Letters'. (ed. Toynbee) July 5, 1755.
65. Quoted in brochure of Chalfont Park Hotel (1921): N. Pevsner, 'Buckinghamshire'. Walpole, July 4, 1760.
66. Walpole: May 7, 1755; Jan. 26, 1762; Oct. 3, 1763.

The Duchess was the granddaughter of the Duke of New-castle, from whom she inherited a large estate, including Welbeck, co. Notts; and after her husband died in 1768, her son, the 3rd Duke of Portland, lived at Welbeck whilst she remained at Bulstrode. 'Mrs. Delany's Letters' (ed. Lady Llanover) (1861–2). 'Mrs. Montague's Letters' (1809–13).

67. Delaney, Sept. 3, 1769.
68. DNB: information from Mr. C. F. Le Mesurier. Mrs. Lybbe Powys, Diary, 13.7.1769.
69. Delany, July 1779.
70. Delany, August 1778.
71. Delany, Nov. 1781: VCH, ii, 223ff, 228.
72. Information from the Queen's Librarian and Mr. L. M. Wulcko: 'Gentleman's Magazine', 1809, 1813. Gott died in 1809. His daughter Sarah married her cousin, Sir Harford Jones.
73. Delany, August 1776: DNB: E. S. Roscoe, 'Penn's Country', p. 39. The 3rd Duke (1738–1809) married a daughter of William, Duke of Devonshire.
74. H. Repton: 'Landscape Gardening' (1840), p. 141. The Duke 'gave leave to all persons to pass through the park, and even encouraged the neighbouring inhabitants to play cricket on the lawn' (p. 602).
75. John Harris, op. cit. Georgiana, Duchess of Devonshire, wrote in 1787 of her agent, Mr. Heaton: 'He has just finished the extricating of the Duke of Portland from distress, and even by useful speculation gives him the prospect of affluence' (Bessborough; 'Georgiana, Duchess of Devonshire').
76. Names from Register, Sessions Records, MR, *passim*. On Overseers Accounts: Records XVIII, 3ff.
77. MR, and information from Mr. Wulcko.

78. Brasenose College archives, Iver. The Woodhill estate (200 acres) was sold by Henry Bulstrode to Sir Sampson Darrell in 1630. There is a sketch-map, drawn by the College Bursar in 1680. In 1778 the house was leased to Mrs. Elizabeth Hutchins. Way mss. (BRO) 57/5, 57/9 are Notices of Sale.

79. VCH, iii, 196: MR 17–20.

80. Glebe terriers, 1703, 1707: Speculum, CSTP, 1705–23 (Lincoln).

81. Bishops' Register (PRO), Foster, 'Oxford Alumni' : M. J. Simmonds, 'Merchant Taylor Fellows of St. John's' : information from the President of St. John's College. A. H. Cocks : 'Church Bells of Bucks.', p. 339.

82. The rampant lion was part of the Trevor crest. William Courtney and his brother Robert had other farms in CSP, and also the Red Lion alehouse (Poor Rate book).

83. W. H. Summers, 'Congregational Churches in S. Bucks. etc.': Urwick, 'Nonconformity in Herts.'

84. Poor Law Union Papers (M.H. 12), vol. 380.

85. Thomas Hibbert, who bought the Chalfont Park estate from Churchill's trustees, was succeeded in 1819 by his brother Robert. Both had been merchants in Jamaica, where Robert married Letitia Nembhard. Robert's first cousin, another Robert, was founder of the Hibbert Trust (DNB and information from Mr. L. Wulcko).

86. Sale catalogue, British Museum Map Room.

87. E. A. and W. Seymour, 'Correspondence of Two Brothers', August 1811. June 1813: 'I hope you have run down to Bulstrode to enjoy its delightful shades. I could wish myself in the lime walk with you.' Amongst Bulstrode papers, BRO, is a sketch-plan of what remained of the house in 1817. Leases: B 2/363, 365. There are particulars prepared for a sale in 1814 in a rent-book kindly lent by Mr. J. Hetherington.

88. H. Janes, 'The Red Barrel': F. C. Cass, 'East Barnet': Annual Register, 1852. 'Windsor and Eton Express', May 15th, 1852.

89. B/4/138.

90. The ladies asked again for a piece of land on the opposite side of the Oxford road, for a sexton's house, 'almost a necessary appendage under the isolated, though valuable, position of the Church', but later withdrew this request, B 4/138, 143.

90a John Bramley-Moore (1800–1886), chairman of Liverpool Docks, had been a notable figure in Brazil (DNB). W. J. Bramley Moore's many books included, in 1912, a life of his cousin, Theodore Pennell, missionary in N.W. India (Venn, Alum. Cantab: B. M. Library Catalogue). Hardy & Sons demolished Bulstrode in 1860, and a new house, designed by Benjamin Ferrey, was built (B 5: Pevsner, Bucks.).

91. Parish Chest: National Society records; Mr. J. Bennell.

92. Redford and Riches, 'Uxbridge', 105. Ogilby's Roadmaps: 1853 Directory: O.S. maps.

93. Presumably the Oakgrove farm land (see above p. 48), which was occupied 1790–1800 by Francis Peter Mallett esq., sheriff of Bucks. in 1793, described in 'Gentleman's Magazine', November 1799, as 'a very respectable person', who had been 'an eminent cabinet maker in Clerkenwell'.

94. Army List, 1840.

95. See E. Mayne Reid, 'Captain Mayne Reid', (1900).

96. Information from Alderman E. L. Colston and other residents.

97. From the first Minute Book of GX Parish Council, by permission.

98. In 1968 the headmaster is Mr. P. E. Rowlett, and a new Infants School has been built in Lovel End.

## ACKNOWLEDGMENT

The publishers gratefully acknowledge the generous assistance of the following firms in the production of this book.

# CHALFONT PARK

## THE TECHNOLOGICAL CENTRE OF THE BRITISH ALUMINIUM COMPANY

*By G. L. Kington, D.Sc.*

*Director, The British Aluminium Co. Ltd.*

Since its early days as a manor house when it was valued in the time of Henry II about 1160 'at £10 and half a mark per annum and 8 loads of barley and a half', Chalfont Park has undergone two major developments. The old mansion was developed to its present form in 1755 by General Charles Churchill, one of whose ancestors had been given the title to the estates by Charles I. The second significant period of development began in 1944 when the property was purchased by The British Aluminium Company as a centre for its research activities. The following 25 years have seen an investment by the company of some half a million pounds and the development of the site as the leading technological centre for aluminium in the country. In this phase, much care has been taken to preserve the old house and many new laboratories and experimental facilities have been built on the site of the old greenhouses and kitchen gardens.

Thus, the present and future of Chalfont is intimately concerned with the fortunes of a major international company in the aluminium industry. The story of The British Aluminium Company is largely the story of world aluminium technology and the development of sources of electrical power. The company's history began in 1894 with the acquisition of the rights to use the Heroult process for manufacturing aluminium and the building of the country's first smelter based on hydroelectric

*P. Heroult.*

generation at Foyers on Loch Ness. This commercial foresight and technological excellence seen at the birth of the company have characterised our activities over three-quarters of a century, and are apparent in the recent decision to build at Invergordon one of the first smelters in the country to be powered from a nuclear source.

The first scientific adviser to the company was Lord Kelvin,

*Kelvin*

then Professor of Natural Philosophy in the University of Glasgow. In those early days the company's processes were controlled by rule-of-thumb, as indeed was much of British industry, and the role of scientifically based research and development was yet to be defined. However, first steps were taken in 1905 with the appointment of a chief chemist, and the first centralised research laboratory was established in Warrington in 1918. Since 1944, the Chalfont Park laboratories have

*Chalfont Park, Gerrards Cross*

grown into a scientific and technological centre of international standing where some 300 people, many of them local residents, find employment.

Technology is a thundering fact of modern civilisation, and scientifically based research and development is the keynote of the technology of The British Aluminium Company. The pursuit of technological innovation in our industry is dependent upon the combined skills of physicists, chemists, metallurgists, mathematicians, and engineers; the Chalfont laboratories house a community of such men all of whom are intimately concerned with improving our processes, broadening the range and quality of our products, and helping customers to use our materials in the most effective manner. The economic prosperity of our country rests in no small measure on the integration of science and industry, on the practical exploitation of scientific understanding, and on the acceptance of the ensuing change. The Chalfont laboratories are in the forefront of this endeavour to achieve a sound technological basis to our economy.

# THE COUNTY GARAGE AND SIXTY YEARS OF MOTORING

*By E. L. Colston, J.P.*

*The County Garage in 1923*

My interest in motoring started before the first World War. I won a 'home made' motor bike in a shilling raffle. It was not particularly reliable and as the carburettor had a habit of catching fire, it necessitated my carrying a bundle of waste to douse the flame.

Next I became, in turn, the owner of an N.S.U., Ariel, Douglas and Triumph. An Indian I wanted, but could never afford.

My first car was a Calthorpe, and this, in the following 40 years, was succeeded by many cars of varied makes.

Perhaps it was not therefore surprising that, on retiring in 1945 from 'big business' I decided to buy a garage and remain in my native village.

The County Garage was originally squeezed between Jewsons Chemist's shop and Frank Nash's hardware store; and just out of the top right-hand corner of the picture above, were the words 'Estd. 1894.'

Also you may be able to detect, in the left-hand window, one car on display and a range of bicycles in the other. In those early days repairs were undertaken for bicycles, cars and also bathchairs!

The County Garage was opened by Mr. William Payne whose main business was selling and repairing bicycles. He had moved there from the centre cottage of St. Hubert's Cottages, by the French Horn, which later became the first 'Little Turret School'. Take a look at the row of cottages, and past, present and future pupils of 'Little Turret' will readily see from whence the name came.

During the war of 1939-45 the County Garage became the first 'outworking' assembly factory of Hoover Ltd., a company with some 10,000 employees, operating for the Ministry of Aircraft Production. Housewives in the neighbourhood worked half-day shifts, mostly on the assembly of small parts. A second 'Assembly Plant' was opened in Station Road. The success of this idea of taking war work to residential areas caught on and resulted in many thousands of additional housewives being employed in war work throughout the country.

There are comparatively few natives of Gerrards Cross who have been able to follow the complete transition from the horse-drawn carriage, bus and coach, and who remember the daily 'carrier' to Uxbridge before the railway was built.

What a transformation it has been from dusty roads and lanes to Tarmacadam surfaces and the building of a residential area of 2-car families—with four garages all intent on giving first-rate service to the residents.

We at the County Garage are proud of our record of service and proud too that we are the oldest established garage in the district.

# WHERE HAVE ALL THE GARDENERS GONE

*By Alan Grey.   Managing Director — Lords of Gerrards Cross*

It was not by accident that beautiful houses came quickly to Gerrards Cross as railway engineers hacked and dug their way westward from Marylebone Station. This was part of the plan. A plan so well executed that the wealthy and famous were soon clamouring for new homes in these beautiful parts of South Buckinghamshire. Within very few years a new 'stock broker belt', still with few rivals, was born.

With beautiful homes there had to be beautiful gardens and Gerrards Cross called widely on an abundant source of willing labour from neighbouring villages. Gardens of grace and charm were hewn virtually by manpower alone. Between two world wars, South Buckinghamshire produced by necessity, and this is the way it always happens, as fine a collection of professional artisan gardeners as anywhere in the country.

Where have all those gardeners gone? Lost for certain in a social revolution, and certainly never to return. Gardens are now measured in parts rather than multiples of acres. Astute and clever planning has given us three or four houses where one stood before. In-filling in Gerrards Cross, with only a few horrible exceptions, has been no disaster. Pretty, smaller houses with smaller but just as lovely gardens exist in abundance all around us today.

Gardening in Gerrards Cross today is a hobby. It is the most popular hobby that exists in our community, partly of course because it exists literally on our doorstep. It is accepted, quite willingly by most, as part of the price we pay to live in lovely rural surroundings.

It is true to say that the resident of Gerrards Cross can still call on a diminishing supply of unskilled labour, available at an alarming cost, to perform some of the more arduous and repetitive work that is necessary in any well run garden. But the gardens remain a symbol of personal endeavour and show evidence to all the results of a rewarding hobby.

How is the miracle achieved? How is it possible in the few short hours available in each week for senior executives and busy professional men to keep gardens of lasting beauty? A simple answer is surely twofold. First, it is of paramount importance that the choice of what to grow and where to grow it, is studied in detail. It is no doubt regretted by some that the herbaceous border and kitchen garden of the past have given way to the more practical cultivation of flowering shrubberies, roses and beautiful lawns. Add to these basic necessities such things as rockeries in natural stone and the enormous profusion of pot and box grown annual flowers and one finds the first key to modern gardening. Secondly, the revolution that has taken place in the development of powered tools together with the aids which science has given for the control of disease in plants, the easy elimination of garden pests and the abundance of artificial fertilisers for the nourishment of the soil, and one finds the key to successful and labour saving maintenance in the modern garden.

The continued success of Lords as a centre where residents can solve most of their gardening problems by asking for and receiving advice, freely given, about what a product or piece of equipment will or will not do, is based we believe on a realisation on our part as to what has happened to gardening over the past twenty years. We believe that we have pioneered in the district all the best mechanical equipment that has become available. We are certain that we have steered some away from gadgets that did not work as they should have done. As company policy we have always shown products of the highest quality, not because they are the most expensive but simply because that is what a discerning public always demands.

In our experience the discerning shopper is more interested in service and advice on an intended purchase than in mere bargain hunting, which has become one of today's national pastimes in other parts. We honestly believe that our service is second to none and our advice is gladly given within the realms of our knowledge. We proudly boast of the small army of residents who return to us time after time for advice on many problems, many of whom pay glowing tribute to the help and advice which we have given in the past.

We honestly believe at Lords that it is a privilege to trade in Gerrards Cross. We talk to many fellow traders who doubt this contention. We believe it is a privilege because we are certain that a retail outlet is only as good as its customers make it, and it will only continue to prosper as long as it offers to an affluent society the quality that that society is entitled to demand, and so long as it backs quality products with sound advice and a first class service.

We believe that the residents of Gerrards Cross can point to us and regrettably at only one or two other privately owned

103

companies as an example of what they are entitled to demand from such retail outlets.

The professional gardener may have left us for ever, but the efforts of the amateur pursuing a rewarding and worthwhile hobby are around us for everyone to enjoy.

We are proud to be associated and of continuing service.

# THE LOVELL CONSTRUCTION GROUP

*by E. W. Segrove F.I.O.B., Chairman*

*The Bellhouse Hotel—a recent Lovell contract*
*Architects: Treadgold, Elsey & Partners*

The Lovell Construction Group—perhaps better known as
'Y. J. LOVELL'—springs from a small country building concern
which came into being at Marlow-on-Thames towards the end
of the 18th century. This business, with its attractive old buildings
and joinery shop, came into the hands of Young James Lovell
in the 1890s, and was carried on by his son, C. P. Lovell, who
opened another branch at Gerrards Cross in 1908. This later
became the company's head office—and remains today the
headquarters of the Group. At the present time, a block of
modern offices is being erected on the Marsham Lane site where
the company has been housed for the past 60 years.

The board of Y. J. Lovell (Holdings) Ltd. includes five direct-
ors who have served the company for more than 25 years, three
of whom joined the original board in 1938—E. F. Burrows

(President), E. W. Segrove (Chairman) and P. H. P. Lovell (Joint Managing Director); the two former have actually completed more than 50 years service.

A large number of staff and operatives, too, have long records of service, and a very happy spirit exists between 'Lovell men' at all levels—perhaps one of the most rewarding features of a life spent in a good business.

Lovells—ranking now as 'National contractors', with operating units in Buckinghamshire, London, Sussex, Devon, Somerset and Hampshire—have carried out a great variety of building works over a wide area in the South and West of England, including schools, Government and public buildings, multi-storey office and residential blocks, churches, hotels and a number of large hospital schemes such as extensions to Guy's, King's College, Middlesex and Royal Sussex hospitals.

We are perhaps concerned here mainly with their contribution to South Bucks in general and Gerrards Cross in particular; so many of the attractive homes in this district are examples of their work and the phrase 'a Lovell House' is a well recognised symbol of quality and character in home-building. It is in many ways regrettable that—perhaps through 'the economies of scale'—comparatively few individual houses are built nowadays to client's order, but Lovells, in developing estate housing and flats at varying price levels, endeavour to maintain standards of design, construction and finish in keeping with the pre-war product.

The company was closely associated between the wars with the building of shopping centres both in Gerrards Cross and at Beaconsfield, while a current development has been the shopping centre and precinct only recently opened at Chalfont St. Peter.

The department for alterations and repair works—plumbing, heating, decorations (repeated at eight other Lovell branches) —provides the house-owner in Gerrards Cross with an efficient "small works" service, offered by an organisation of considerable substance and with long experience in the building world.

The Group is proud of its training schemes which prepare selected young men for senior positions in various branches of the trade; it is quite normal for members of staff to attend weekly or fortnightly courses at universities or colleges, and the ambitious and hard-working student—who in many cases may have come from the ranks of the apprentices—can make his choice from a number of fine opportunities in the construction

106

world. Today, there is particular scope for the well-educated boy who is looking for a deeply satisfying and rewarding career.

Certainly, the name of LOVELL stands high in the construction industry, and the Group now employs more than 2,500 staff and operatives, which, with the aid of extensive mechanisation and the adoption of modern management techniques, has enabled the company to attain a turnover exceeding £12,000,000 per annum.

# GERRARDS CROSS MEMORIAL CENTRE

The Memorial Centre on East Common is the home of the Gerrards Cross Community Association. The building was a former vicarage, as may be deduced from the footpath leading across the common to St. James' Church, and was acquired just after the 1939-45 war, as a memorial to the fallen.

The intention of its founders was that it should be a living memorial, and the hub of community activities in the parish.

This aim has been achieved in many respects. The Community Association, registered as a charity under the 1960 Act, has more than 1,000 members and well over this number pass through its doors every week to take part in the activities of their favourite club or to join a class sponsored by the Centre or the local educational authority.

The choice is wide—badminton and bridge, music and photography, art and antiques, drama and flower arrangement, English and foreign languages and many others.

The Association is governed by a Community Council of some seventy members, who are either elected by the membership or nominees of affiliated organisations. There are representatives of national organisations, local authorities, churches, local societies, sports and social clubs. The Council provides a useful forum for matters of importance in the parish and a wealth of

108

experience is available in their discussions of local affairs.

The management of the Memorial Centre is delegated to an Executive Committee, which is elected by the Community Council, with the assistance of a full-time warden and staff. There are a number of sub-committees to attend to such matters as Education, Finance and Publicity.

Although most activities are sectional, there are some in which many of the members gather together. At the annual Summer Fair, which has many of the attributes of a village feast day, members of most affiliated clubs and societies may be seen working together to provide a happy day for the local community and, incidentally, a profitable one for the development fund of the Association.

In the early days of the Association a few families met together in the grounds of the Centre to celebrate Guy Fawkes Day and this has become over the years a gathering of several thousand people, with a magnificent display of fireworks, followed by an enormous bonfire with roast chestnuts and other seasonal fare.

The premises adjacent to the Memorial Centre were erected as a memorial to the fallen of the 1914-18 war and a plaque recording their names occupies the prime position in this building designed by the famous architect, Sir Edwin Lutyens.

It seemed to many residents of the parish that the two memorials, since they had almost identical objects, should be brought closer together. This has now been partly accomplished by a combination of retirement and appointment of trustees so that both trusts are held by the same individuals, who lease the First World War Memorial premises to the Community Association.

A new Youth Centre, built in the grounds, was opened in 1967 by Sir Robert Bellinger, during his term as Lord Mayor of London.

The integration of the two memorials having begun, it is now the intention of the Community Association to seek ways of further improving the facilities available on both sites, so that this attractive corner of the parish may continue worthily to portray the fostering and furtherance of those arts and exercises healthful and enriching to body and mind, in loyalty to the memory of those who gave their lives for our national heritage in the two World Wars.

# LET THERE BE LIGHT . . .

*by Harold E. Percivall (Managing Director of Percivall's Ltd.)*

The people of Gerrards Cross and Chalfont St. Peter still go to the village to do their shopping. To the town dwellers of cities and suburbia this conjures up an impression of 'ye olde worlde', oil lamps, log fires, a general store and gas lighted streets and lanes. Yet nothing could be further from the truth than to think that the price we all pay for living in this attractive area, in a village community, means forfeiting the advantages which make life more comfortable and safer.

Without losing their outward charm, most houses in our two villages are equipped with the most modern and up-to-date electric appliances, and electricity has become the very life blood on which our community thrives. In bringing this about, my family and I have given our service to Gerrards Cross and Chalfont St. Peter for many decades. Percivall's is a family business and we like to think that our many employees, technicians, electricians, maintenance engineers and sales staff are part of that family. In an age, where large business ventures and companies replace the personal service of the local shopkeeper and craftsman, we are proud to be among the few family businesses left in Gerrards Cross. As the head of my family and the business I take personal responsibility for the service we render. Whether we are asked to rewire a four hundred year old cottage, a private house built in this century or equip a factory, offices and new schools with all the necessary electrical appliances, our care and personal interest we take in each job never varies. No job has ever been too large or too small for us.

Most of all I value the confidence the people of Gerrards Cross and Chalfont St. Peter have been placing in us when we are called upon to advise them on the many problems which can arise in homes and businesses alike; it does not matter whether the television set has gone wrong, a table lamp needs fixing or a whole building needs rewiring, we know that we can advise them and help them. The retail section of my business takes care of anything from the lamp bulb to the most sophisticated electrical machinery which turns any kitchen into a dream.

We are proud to be part of this thriving community and, not without justification, we say: Let there be light, and warmth and comfort . . .

110

# WEST END SHOPPING IN BUCKS

I suppose that we all like personal attention, and indeed some shops have founded their reputation on just this, although, of course, a considerable knowledge of the trade concerned must accompany it. Such a shop is **Trudels of Gerrards Cross.**

One might be inclined to pass this shop as just another hardware store, but this is one with a difference, for not only does Mrs. Lay stock all the usual kitchen equipment but a host of other things as well. She has had long experience in her trade, and a couple of years back started up her well laid out store in Pack-horse Road, attracting a wide clientele both by her policy of personal attention and from the remarkable display of excellent items in the shop. This made my visit much longer than I had expected.

Everything that anyone has ever invented for either the kitchen or the table seems to be available, and I feel sure that if I ever felt the urge to invest in an old fashioned knife cleaner or a scrubbing board Mrs. Lay could get it for me, even as she will get you anything from a lawn mower to a deep-freeze, although refrigerators and the like are kept in stock.

Most of the good makes of china and glass are available and all sorts of kitchen stuff and gadgets. I found the display of stainless steel very alluring, with all the wonderful shapes and designs that are available nowadays. The English Old Hall and the Scandinavian Seaware both have many attractions in the tableware department, including coffee pots and sugar bowls. Although I prefer to do my cooking in the kitchen, many of us like to flambé things at the table, and this is where the Spring Gourmet Line of fondue dishes come into their own. Most of them are in copper, but there are some in ceramics as well, all with the proper braziers to go with them, although, of course the individual items can be bought separately. Then there are the porcelain enamel cast iron casseroles and frying pans from Nacco and Copco of Denmark, and similar decorated ones from Sital of Italy. These, with their attractive shapes and bright colours, intended to be used straight from the oven to the table, really bring a bit of imaginative colour into things—and they are easy to clean. I was attracted, too, by the Sheba Line in both kitchen and table cutlery, very up to date in appearance, but of pleasing shapes and great utility. I hope someone will give me the set of six kitchen knives in their aforomosia holdster.

*Reprinted from 'Bucks Life'*

# LONDON BOROUGH OF LEWISHAM

## LIBRARIES DEPARTMENT

Books must be returned on or before the last date stamped below or on the date card. Fines on overdue books will be charged:— ½d per day for the first week (1d minimum), 1d per day for the second week. 2d per day thereafter.

Books are renewable by phone, letter or personal call unless required by another reader.

ALL LIBRARIES are closed on Sundays, Good Friday, Christmas Day, Bank Holidays, and the Saturdays prior to Bank Holidays.